The Man of the Crowd

THE MAN
OF THE
CROWD

EDGAR
ALLAN POE
AND THE CITY

SCOTT
PEEPLES

**PHOTOGRAPHS BY
MICHELLE VAN PARYS**

PRINCETON UNIVERSITY PRESS

PRINCETON AND OXFORD

Requests for permission to reproduce material from this work should be sent to permissions@press.princeton.edu

Published by Princeton University Press
41 William Street, Princeton, New Jersey 08540
6 Oxford Street, Woodstock, Oxfordshire OX20 1TR

press.princeton.edu

LCCN 2020020492
ISBN 9780691182407
ISBN (e-book) 9780691212081

British Library Cataloging-in-Publication Data is available

Editorial: Anne Savarese and Jenny Tan
Production Editorial: Leslie Grundfest and Debbie Tegarden
Text Design: Leslie Flis
Production: Erin Suydam
Publicity: Jodi Price and Amy Stewart

Jacket/Cover Credit: Michelle Van Parys

This book has been composed in Sabon text with Aachen and Franklin Gothic display

Printed on acid-free paper. ∞

Printed in the United States of America

10 9 8 7 6 5 4 3 2 1

For Jerry Kennedy

Contents

Abbreviations

Throughout the text, Poe's works are cited parenthetically with the following abbreviations:

D = *Doings of Gotham*, edited by Jacob E. Spannuth and Thomas Ollive Mabbott (Folcroft, PA: Folcroft Library Editions, [1929] 1974).

ER = *Essays and Reviews*, edited by G. R. Thompson (New York: Library of America, 1984).

EU = *Eureka*, edited by Stuart Levine and Susan F. Levine (Urbana: University of Illinois Press, 2004).

CL = *The Collected Letters of Edgar Allan Poe*, 2 vols., 3rd ed.; edited by John Ward Ostrom, Burton R. Pollin, and Jeffrey A. Savoye (New York: Gordian, 2008).

P = *Complete Poems*, edited by Thomas Ollive Mabbott (Urbana: University of Illinois Press, [1969] 2000).

T = *Tales and Sketches*, 2 vols., edited by Thomas Ollive Mabbott (Urbana: University of Illinois Press, [1978] 2000).

The Man of the Crowd

Introduction

NO PLACE LIKE HOME

In 1823, when Edgar Allan Poe was a restless fourteen-year-old living with his foster family in Richmond, Virginia, a well-known actor named John Howard Payne wrote the lyrics to what would become one of the most popular songs of the nineteenth century:

> Mid pleasures and palaces, though we may roam,
> Be it ever so humble, there's no place like home,
> A charm from the sky seems to hallow us there,
> Which, seek through the world, is ne're met with
>> elsewhere,
>
>> Home, home, sweet, sweet home!
>> There's no place like home, oh there's no place like
>>> home!
>
> An exile from home splendor dazzles in vain,
> Oh, give me my lowly thatched cottage again,
> The birds singing gaily that come at my call,
> Give me them with that peace of mind, dearer than all.
>
>> Home, home, sweet, sweet home!
>> There's no place like home, oh there's no place like
>>> home!

Coincidentally, Payne had appeared onstage opposite Poe's mother throughout April and May 1809, just after Edgar was born.[1] Because his mother died before he turned three,

Edgar probably never knew of this connection to Payne, but he surely knew the song "Home Sweet Home," which was a sheet-music blockbuster performed in parlors and on stages throughout his lifetime.

Like most songs about home, Payne's lyric is really about *longing* for home. It first appeared in the operetta *Clari; or, the Maid of Milan*, where it was sung by the unfortunate title character after she left her home and fell prey to a wicked seducer. Appropriately, the American Payne composed the song while living in Paris. He wrote to his loved ones around the same time, "My yearnings toward Home become stronger as the term of my exile lengthens . . . I feel the want of you, parts of myself, in this strange world, for though I am naturalized to vagabondage, still it is *but* vagabondage . . . I long for a home about me."[2] Payne's song, and the endless stream of popular music evoking the same longing, resonated with generations of Americans who found themselves somewhere other than "home."

In the first half of the nineteenth century, somewhere-other-than-home was likely to be a city such as the ones where Edgar Poe spent most of his life. The years 1820–50—three-fourths of Poe's lifetime—saw "the most rapid urbanization in American history," according to historian Daniel Walker Howe.[3] Driven by manufacturing and trade, American cities grew dramatically, populated by young people who migrated from family farms as well as by European immigrants, mainly from Ireland, England, and Germany. The number of American towns with populations over ten thousand went from six to sixty in less than fifty years.[4] Of course, a person can have more than one home in a lifetime, and yet the notion of a "homeland" as a place to which one is emotionally anchored, through ancestry, memory, and sentiment, persists even today. Especially in the sentimental culture of antebellum America, "home" evoked not just a "lowly thatched cottage" but also the rural community that surrounded it; the city, by contrast, was a place of estrangement. Geographer Yi-Fu Tuan describes home or homeland as the center of a person's spatial system: "The stars are perceived to move around one's abode; home is the focal point of a cosmic structure. . . . [T]o abandon it would be hard to imagine."[5] Living far away from that center, that focal point, is what the song "Home Sweet Home" is about.

Poe was not one of those who left the farm for the factory, but, with the exception of a few years spent in college and the army, he lived in cities his entire life. And, as the son of actors whose companies performed up and down the eastern seaboard, Poe was not only a child of the city but a child of transience, constantly moving from place to place. If Payne felt exiled, or "naturalized to vagabondage," Poe was born into vagabondage. Throughout his childhood, living with the Allan family of Richmond, he was acutely aware of his orphan status, as he was never legally adopted or included in his foster father's will. Including changes of address within cities, Poe relocated approximately thirty-five times in his forty-year life. Although he called the city of Richmond home as a young man, for most if his life, *home*—homeland or cosmic focal point—was experienced not as something lost but something he never really knew. Poe was not so much uprooted as unrooted.

In his vagabondage as well as his struggles with poverty, Poe differed from most "major" American authors—at least most major white authors—of his time. Poe's contemporary Nathaniel Hawthorne, for instance, was very much rooted in Salem, Massachusetts, and, except for an extended residence in Europe from 1853 to 1860, lived in New England his entire life. Though never wealthy, Hawthorne's living conditions were solidly middle class, and he had a support system that included a United States president, Franklin

Pierce. Harriet Beecher Stowe, who lived twice as long as Poe, was born in Litchfield, Connecticut, and died in nearby Hartford, where she spent her last thirty-six years. When she lived in other cities (Cincinnati, Ohio, and Brunswick, Maine), she and her family stayed for over a decade, in comfortable, spacious homes. James Fenimore Cooper, who was born two decades before Poe but outlived him by three years, is closely associated with Cooperstown, New York, the town his father established, and where he spent his last fifteen years. In between, he lived prosperously in New York City and, for seven years, in Europe. All of the other figureheads of the "American Renaissance" were rooted in a specific city, town, or region, even if they did not spend their entire lives there—Concord, Massachusetts, for Ralph Waldo Emerson and Henry David Thoreau; New York City for Walt Whitman and Herman Melville; and Amherst, Massachusetts, for Emily Dickinson. Whitman and Melville experienced economic hardship as children, and Thoreau chose a Spartan economic life as an adult, but none of them experienced the career-long poverty that Poe did, and none of them moved nearly as often. Poe's rootless life might not have been unique among poor yet ambitious men of his time, but it seems to have been quite unlike that of his canonical contemporaries.

This book is an attempt to tell the story of that unrooted life with a distinct focus on the American cities where Poe lived for extended periods of time: Richmond, Baltimore, Philadelphia, and New York. Of course, Poe's life does not fit neatly into chapters set in those four cities. There is also Boston, his birthplace; London, where he spent five years as a boy with the Allans; Charlottesville, Virginia, where he was a student; West Point, New York, where he was a cadet; Sullivan's Island, South Carolina, and Old Point Comfort, Virginia, where he was an enlisted man. Moreover, after leaving Richmond in 1827, he would return several times to visit and would relocate there for over a year, in 1835–37. He lived in New York on two separate occasions, though little is known about the first, shorter stay. While I describe all of those departures and arrivals, in this book I will incorporate them into chapters anchored by the cities that define distinct periods of Poe's life, then conclude with a chapter chronicling the last year and a half of that life, a period defined less by residence than by travel. *The Man of the Crowd*, then, is a compact biography of Poe that reconsiders his work and career in light of his itinerancy and his relationship to the cities where he lived.

By emphasizing his physical and social environment, I hope to counter an old but still pervasive impression of Poe as an isolated figure, a "nowhere man" who lived somewhere in America but perhaps did not belong there, who was oblivious to his surroundings.[6] "There is no place," wrote W. H. Auden, "in any of [his stories] for the human individual as he actually exists in space and time."[7] The poet Richard Wilbur, an astute interpreter of Poe, would go even further, arguing that he "sees the poetic soul as *at war with the mundane physical world*; and that warfare is Poe's fundamental subject."[8] And here is Galway Kinnell, contrasting Poe to his contemporary Walt Whitman: "Poe's poetry was the poetry of a blind man, a man who was imagining some realm somewhere else."[9] Such claims are understandable, given that most of Poe's poetry and much of his best-known fiction takes place in unspecified or imaginary locations. Poe neither provides the coordinates of the "kingdom by the sea" where Annabel Lee is buried, nor indicates the town nearest the House of Usher—nor, for that matter, the country in which Usher resides. When he does set a story in an actual place, it's likely to be a place he did not know firsthand, such as Paris in the three stories featuring the original literary detective C. Auguste Dupin.

Although Poe did not know Paris firsthand, the Dupin stories exemplify his fascination with "the city" as a phenomenon. The modern detective story, which Poe originated, could only have developed in an urban milieu: though urbanization is not a necessary condition for crime, by Poe's time cities and crime were closely associated. Increasingly, cities established police forces to catch criminals and solve crimes—and thereby to serve as foils for amateur sleuths like M. Dupin. Cities were populated by "strangers," a condition that both enabled crime (anonymity is the norm, and there is no shortage of victims) and created suspicion (when nearly everyone is a stranger, anyone could be a criminal).[10] And, perhaps most significant, cities had newspapers, which, especially with the rise of the penny press, publicized crime and made it possible for an "armchair detective" to operate. In "The Murders in the Rue Morgue," which I discuss in chapter 3, Dupin gleans information about the killing from the newspaper and uses a newspaper advertisement to lure the criminal. Its sequel, "The Mystery of Marie Rogêt," is essentially a conversation with newspaper reports and speculation about a murder.

"Marie Rogêt" is a true tale of the city, though it might be hard to tell which city. Poe wrote the story while living in Philadelphia; he set it in Paris, but it follows the investigation of a recent murder in New York. He first pitched the tale to a Boston editor:

The story is based upon the assassination of Mary Cecilia Rogers, which created so vast an excitement, some months ago, in New-York. I have, however, handled my design in a manner altogether *novel* in literature. I have imagined a series of nearly exact *coincidences* occurring in Paris. A young grisette, one Marie Rogêt, has been murdered under precisely similar circumstances with Mary Rogers. Thus, under pretence of showing how Dupin (the hero of "The Rue Morgue") unraveled the mystery of Marie's assassination, I, in reality, enter into a very long and rigorous analysis of the New-York tragedy. No point is omitted. I examine, each by each, the opinions and arguments of the press upon the subject, and show that this subject has been, hitherto, *unapproached*. In fact, I believe not only that I have demonstrated the fallacy of the general idea—that the girl was the victim of a gang of ruffians—but have *indicated the assassin* in a manner which will give renewed impetus to investigation. (T 2:718)

Both the Boston *Notion* and Baltimore's *Saturday Visiter* took a pass on the sequel to "Rue Morgue," but Poe managed to place it in a New York magazine called the *Ladies' Companion*. A freelancer with connections to periodicals in all the major eastern cities, he was used to pitching his work, getting rejected, and weighing the relative benefits of high visibility or decent pay. With "Marie Rogêt," Poe had written a timely tale with a looming expiration date. He was writing about what people on the street were talking about— in this case, a grisly unsolved murder—but the story also shows him intervening in a real-life mystery through the medium of the periodical press, itself a creature of the modern city and the center of Poe's professional life. At the peak of his career, Poe considered himself "essentially a Magazinist": a title that describes his professional life more accurately than the terms usually applied to him today: fiction writer, poet, critic, editor (L 1:470). He was all of those things and more (journalist, essayist), but with rare exceptions, he made his name, and his living, providing content for magazines published in the major eastern cities of Richmond, Baltimore, Philadelphia, New York, and Boston.

In the case of "Marie Rogêt," Dupin does not feel the need to visit the scene of the crime or to interview any witnesses.

Like his creator, Poe, Dupin relies on newspapers. Poe quotes extensively from New York papers (renamed with French titles) to review the leading theories and to set up Dupin's—that is, his own—response. Although the crime itself was real, Poe's story is very much a product of print culture, with one writer responding in public to other writers. Poe does not develop Marie/Mary's character or anyone else's. He does not solve the mystery of Marie Rogêt, either: Poe "indicated the assassin" to be an unnamed, swarthy naval officer, an acquaintance of Marie/Mary, and even *that* claim turned out to be inaccurate. Between the second and third, final installment of "Marie Rogêt," new evidence in the Mary Rogers case emerged in the form of a deathbed confession by one Frederika Loss, who confirmed an already prevalent theory that Mary had died from complications during an abortion. At that point Poe couldn't win: if he changed his story to conclude that Mary died during a botched abortion procedure, he would be seen as cheating, but if he stayed the course, he'd be seen as having spent a lot of time and effort to reach a false conclusion. So, after delaying the publication of the final installment by a month, Poe punted, merely arguing against an already debunked hypothesis—that Mary had been abducted and killed by a street gang.[11]

"The Mystery of Marie Rogêt" is not one of Poe's greatest accomplishments: in the one story in which Dupin attempts to solve a crime that was not plotted by his creator, he comes up short. The "long and rigorous analysis" Poe promised is long indeed, and a bit tedious for most modern readers. And yet, in its focus on urban crime, its attempt to blend journalism with fiction in order to intervene in a current controversy, "Marie Rogêt" shows us a Poe very unlike his popular image as an isolated, mad genius "at war with the physical world."

Poe's stories told by killers have a decidedly urban feel, as well, despite not being set in a specific city. In "The Tell-Tale Heart," the police suspect foul play because neighbors had heard the old man's shriek; the street is densely populated enough for them to hear it, and too densely populated for the killer to risk moving the body from the house. In "The Black Cat," the narrator twice calls attention to the "dense crowd" that "filled" his garden on the night his house catches fire (T 2:853). And in this story, too, the killer buries the victim on the premises to avoid "the risk of being observed by the neighbors" (T 2:856).[12]

Indeed, to nineteenth-century readers, cities were dangerous, mysterious places: they were constantly changing, easy to get lost in, and hard to comprehend. One of the most popular fictional genres of the mid-nineteenth century was the "city mystery" novel, which highlighted crime and vice, particularly prostitution and extramarital sex, as well as theft, gambling, and drunkenness. These novels were "mysteries" not in the whodunit sense, but, rather, in their insistence on exposing illicit activity usually hidden from view. Not coincidentally, one of the earliest and most popular American city mystery novels, *The Quaker City*, was written by Poe's friend George Lippard, whom he met in Philadelphia in the early 1840s.

While living in Philadelphia, Poe wrote the story that lends this book its title. In "The Man of the Crowd," which I discuss in chapter 3, the story's narrator spends an entire night following another man through the crowded streets of London. A creature of the city, the man keeps moving, always part of the crowd. The pursuer provides a clinical description of the people, the streets, the whole nocturnal scene of the city, while focusing on this one man who, paradoxically, stands out for the extent to which he blends in or embodies the crowd. While the title of my book implicitly refers to Poe, I don't mean that Poe blended in with the crowd—far from it. Poe did not love crowds and was consistently dismissive of "the mob," yet he was much more a product of the city than his reputation suggests. Not only did he live in rapidly growing cities for most of his life; his livelihood depended on appealing to "the crowd," the increasingly urban consumers of magazine literature. And like the man of the crowd, Poe had to keep moving: literally, he walked the streets of every city he knew, from rented house to magazine office, from magazine office to another writer's house, and, too often, to a nearby saloon or bar. But, in a broader sense, too, he was almost constantly on the move. Poe's attachments to specific places were temporary, and he understood them to be so.

The narrator of "The Man of the Crowd" is both fascinated and mystified by his subject, concluding that he is "a book that will not permit itself to be read." I know how he feels: I've been following Poe around from city to city for some time, and he remains enigmatic, always one step ahead. Even so, in these pages I've tried to offer more than a fleeting glimpse of a man in motion; I've tried to depict Poe as a man living and working, enjoying professional victories and frustrating losses, in the cities that were increasingly coming to define modern American life. Like his fictional man of the crowd, Poe was accustomed to movement, and acquainted with alienation.

This is not a work of academic criticism or a comprehensive biography or complete overview of the Poe canon. I have not skipped over any major events in Poe's life, but, in emphasizing where Poe was and what it was like for him to live there, I have spent relatively less time on other aspects of his personal life and his writing process. The works I discuss also reflect my focus on Poe's urban experience: for that reason, I devote more attention, for instance, to "The

Murders in the Rue Morgue" and the journalistic series "Doings of Gotham" than I do to "The Fall of the House of Usher" and "The Black Cat." But, while I don't discuss every major work, I have been struck by how much of Poe's writing does connect to the simple fact that his life and career were inseparable from the development of the American city. Poe craved success as a writer and editor—his career-long ambition was to control his own magazine—and there was no way to separate that ambition from the series of cities to which he moved, ending with New York. He encountered true poverty in Baltimore in the early 1830s, and it followed him throughout his adult life, showing up in his stories in various guises. His drinking problem cannot be blamed on city life, but the cities he lived in certainly offered opportunities and occasions to give in to that dangerous impulse.

As these chapters demonstrate, Poe was ambivalent about urban life and about the places where he lived and worked. When he could manage it, especially after his wife became ill, he tried to live on the outskirts, close enough to ply his trade as an editor and a freelance writer but at a somewhat safe distance from the noise, foul air, and temptations of the city center. Still, at a time when suburbs were a new concept and public transportation was slow and somewhat expensive, life outside the city tended to leave Poe personally and professionally isolated. He had a number of priorities when it came to choosing where to live, some of which were in conflict with each other: low rent, proximity to local publishing centers, and a healthy, semirural environment. It's no wonder he moved as often as he did.

Poe was one of the most inventive and original writers of his time. But, exceptional as he was, he was also, in many ways, a typical American white man of the first half of the nineteenth century: he was free to move, to pursue a dream, but frustrated by low pay and limited career options. Other men owned the businesses he worked for. Other people owned the houses he lived in. So he kept moving and tried to make a decent life for his family. His legacy in literature and popular culture is wide ranging and profound, yet in his lifetime he must have felt that he never quite made it. He achieved fame and admiration for his writing but he never gained control over his career. He found and held on to a loving family, but he never found a place to rest. Wherever he was, it was no place like home.

CHAPTER 1

Richmond (1809–1827)

In the spring of 1827, eighteen-year-old Edgar Allan Poe was leaving home. In a letter sent across town to his wealthy foster father, John Allan, on March 19, he announced his intention "to leave your house and indeavor [*sic*] to find some place in this wide world, where I will be treated—*not* as *you* have treated me" (L 1:10). His strained relationship with Allan had reached a breaking point following a year at the University of Virginia, during which the young student had accumulated considerable debt. And now that he had left his foster father's house—or been cast out—he was writing both to declare his independence and to ask for help, to "defray the expences [*sic*] of my passage to some of the Northern cit[i]es & then support me for one month" (L 1:11). That undiplomatic combination, of upbraiding Allan while asking him for money, would recur throughout Poe's quest for independence over the next several years. But the eighteen-year-old correctly saw this moment as a turning point. Though Poe was born in Boston, had lived with the Allan family in England and Scotland from 1815 to 1820, and spent most of 1826 in Charlottesville, Richmond was the closest thing to a hometown he would ever have. By breaking with John Allan and leaving Richmond (though still asking for financial support), Poe was making the transition to adulthood.

Edgar had grown up in Richmond not because his family had settled there but because his mother had died there. Elizabeth (or Eliza) Arnold Hopkins was a beautiful and popular actress and singer who had performed to appreciative audiences up and down the East Coast since childhood. Having married at fifteen, Eliza became a widow at nineteen, and several months later married David Poe, a Baltimore actor less talented than herself. The couple spent long theatrical seasons in Boston with shorter runs in other eastern cities, as Eliza juggled a busy stage career with motherhood, giving birth to two sons: William Henry Leonard (known as Henry) in January 1807, and Edgar in January 1809. By the time her daughter, Rosalie, was born in December 1810, David had abandoned the stage and the family, frustrated by financial difficulties and cruel reviews that contrasted with his wife's favorable notices; it didn't help that he very likely had a drinking problem.[1] Edgar barely knew his father. He spent his first three years in at least six different cities, including Boston, New York, Baltimore (where as an infant he lived with David's parents for about six months), Richmond, Norfolk, and Charleston—wherever Eliza's career took them. Little is known about Edgar's early childhood except that it was marked by itinerancy and instability.

Suffering from symptoms that suggest tuberculosis, Eliza spent her last months performing in Richmond, where she was well known and appreciated, and died in December of that year. David Poe probably died around the same time, although the circumstances of his death are unknown.[2] Edgar's brother, Henry, was already being raised by David's parents in Baltimore; Edgar and Rosalie were taken in by two prominent Richmond families who had befriended Eliza. Rosalie went with Jane and William Mackenzie, while Edgar was fostered, but not formally adopted, by a childless couple: John Allan, a thirty-two-year-old merchant, and his twenty-six-year-old wife, Frances. Edgar grieved heavily for his mother, who had been the one stable presence in his life, and he grew up with a constant awareness of his status as a foster child. Richmond was not quite his hometown, just as the Allans were not quite his parents.

In the 1810s and 1820s, Richmond was small but rapidly growing: its population would multiply from 5,737 in 1800 to 20,153 in 1840. Throughout Poe's lifetime it ranked third in size among southern cities—behind New Orleans and Charleston—and in 1820 it was the tenth largest city in the United States by total (enslaved and free) population.[3] In addition to its political significance as the capital of a large, nationally influential state, Richmond became Virginia's center of commerce and industry in the first half of the nineteenth century, thanks largely to its proximity to the coast and access to a network of inland waterways. Tobacco and wheat were processed in Richmond's factories, as were coal and iron. Writing in 1824, Henry Cogswell Knight described the city's atmosphere as "impregnated with the dense murky affluvia of coal-smoke, which begrimes the pores of the skin, and affects respiration."[4] Two decades later, Alexander MacKay, writing for a London newspaper, contrasted the "closeness and dinginess" of Richmond's business district with its "elegant and airy" suburbs, as viewed from the neoclassical Capitol building designed by Thomas Jefferson:

> In the immediate foreground is the town, the greater portion of which is so directly underneath you that it almost seems as if you could leap into it. Before you is the James River, tumbling in snowy masses over successive ledges of rock, its channel being divided by several islands, which are shrouded in foliage, and imbedded in foaming rapids. To the south of the river, an extensive vista opens up, spreading far to the right and left, cleared in some places, but, generally speaking, mantled in the most luxuriant vegetation. The

Figure 1.1 *View of Richmond from Church Hill*, lithograph by E. Sachse, mid-nineteenth century. (Courtesy of the Library of Congress, Prints and Photographs Division, LC-DIG-pga-02597.)

scene is one over which the stranger may well linger, particularly on a bright summer's day, skipping from the distant Alleghenies, carrying the fragrant perfume of the magnolia and honeysuckle on their wings.[5]

Richmond was a topographical and cultural hybrid, a small, grimy city embedded in a lush southern landscape, dominated by businessmen and lawyers but economically dependent on, and geographically surrounded by, slaveholding plantation owners, the traditional Virginia gentry.[6]

Poe's foster father typified the Richmond businessman. An orphan himself who had emigrated from Scotland, John Allan ran an import-export firm with his partner, Charles Ellis, trading heavily in tobacco but importing everything from crosscut saws to Irish linen.[7] Though hard-working and proud, Allan was not entirely self-made: his career was guided and financially supported by his uncle William Galt,

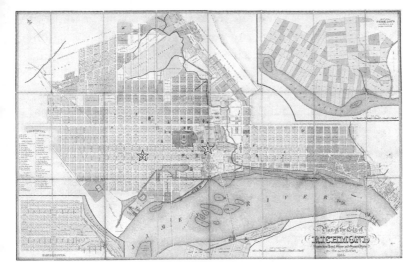

Figure 1.2 Development plan of Richmond, Virginia, 1835. The locations of the Allan home on "Tobacco Alley" (1) and their later mansion, Moldavia (2), are marked. (Special Collections, University of Virginia Library.)

whose own business acumen had made him one of the wealthiest men in Virginia. And it didn't hurt that Allan had married into an aristocratic Virginia family, the Valentines.[8] Edgar's more indulgent foster mother, Frances Keeling Valentine Allan, was about the same age his mother would have been, and, like Eliza Poe, beautiful and frail. Edgar, who had lived on the road with acting companies for his first three years, now found himself in comfortable surroundings with an indulgent surrogate mother, but also under the supervision of a self-righteous foster father who cherished what would come to be known as the Protestant work ethic. When the Allans added Edgar to their household, they lived on the northeast corner of Thirteenth Street and East Main, above the Ellis and Allan business office, a common arrangement even for prosperous families. Poe spent these formative years, from age three to six, living in the midst of the commercial district of a rapidly developing city, within a block of Capitol Square, the political center of Virginia but also a spot from which one could experience the visual and sensual feast described by Alexander MacKay. The Allans doted on young Edgar, who began to receive formal schooling, had access to books, and became acquainted with Richmond society, reportedly delighting guests at social gatherings with precocious skills in recitation.[9]

When Edgar was six, John Allan temporarily relocated the family—Frances, Edgar, and Frances's older sister Anne (known as "Aunt Nancy")—to England, where Ellis and Allan opened a branch of their expanding business. After a month-long ocean voyage and several weeks in Allan's native Scotland, the family settled in London for the next five years; by the time they left, Poe had spent more of his life there than in any other city. The Allans moved into the fashionable Bloomsbury district, at 47 Southampton Row and, later, 39 Southampton Row, in the immediate vicinity of Bloomsbury Square, Russell Square, and, intriguingly, the British Museum (then located in Montague House). Three afternoons a week, admission was free; Poe would have had many opportunities to explore classical treasures and see the famous Rosetta Stone, which had been installed in 1802.[10] Already the most populous city in the world, with over a million inhabitants, London must have been mind-blowing to a young boy from Richmond.[11] Charles Lamb had enumerated the city's attractions in a letter to William Wordsworth about fifteen years earlier:

> The lighted shops of the Strand and Fleet Street, the innumerable trades, tradesmen, and customers, coaches, waggons, playhouses; all the bustle and wickedness round about Covent Garden; the very women of the Town; the watchmen, drunken scenes, rattles; life awake, if you are awake, at all

hours of the night, the impossibility of being dull in Fleet
Street; the crowds, the very dirt and mud, the sun shining
upon houses and pavements, the print-shops, the old book-
stalls, parsons cheapening books, coffee-houses, steams of
soups coming from kitchens, the pantomimes—London itself a pantomime and a masquerade.[12]

Surely a boy Poe's age would not appreciate this "masquerade" in the way Lamb did, but the sensory feast must have
made a strong impression on the imaginative youngster, one
that no American city could match.

It was a different world indeed. Though it would seem
ethnically homogenous compared to its twenty-first-century
self, London was already quite diverse, with African and
Asian enclaves as well as immigrants from Ireland and the
European continent.[13] The effects of industrialization and
problems synonymous with poverty and overcrowding were
significantly more pronounced in London than anywhere in
the United States—and, although the Allans lived comfort-
ably throughout their stay, Poe could not have been completely shielded from the gritty realities of modern urban
life. In fact, the notoriously crowded "bustle and wicked-
ness round about Covent Garden" and the sordid "rooker-
ies" of Seven Dials lay within a mile to the southwest of the
Allan residence.[14] Charles Lamb's affectionate portrait notwithstanding, many Londoners (and visitors) no doubt sec-
onded Percy Shelley's assessment in *Peter Bell the Third*,
published in 1819:

Hell is a city much like London–

   A populous and a smoky city;
There are all sorts of people undone,
And there is little or no fun done;
   Small justice shown, and still less pity.[15]

Rampant poverty, crime, and contagious diseases were part of London's social fabric in the 1810s.[16] Charles Dickens, three years younger than Poe, grew up in the same environment (about a mile from the Allans' residence, in fact), and his novels depicting the city's complexities, especially the travails of its lower classes, would impress upon millions of readers the image of London as *the* modern city. The adult Edgar Poe would pay tribute to Dickens— arguably plagiarizing him—with "The Man of the Crowd," his tale of urban paranoia (which I discuss in chapter 3), and he would take pride in forecasting the outcome of Dickens's serialized novel *Barnaby Rudge* and in meeting the great man in Philadelphia during his American tour of 1842.[17]

While young Edgar absorbed many of London's sights and sounds over five years, he probably saw less of the British Museum, Southampton Row, and his foster parents than he would have liked. Early on, Allan had tried sending his six-year-old ward to be educated in Scotland, but Edgar rebelled: sulking, refusing to do his schoolwork, and threatening to find his own way back to London. The Allans then placed him at a boarding school closer to home—run by "the Misses Dubourg," sisters of John Allan's bookkeeper and copyist—on Sloane Street in Chelsea.[18] At the Dubourgs' he was just a few miles from "home," but he likely saw his foster parents only on weekends, at best. After two years, Poe began boarding at a school farther from central London, in the northern suburb of Stoke Newington. At the Manor House School, run by the Reverend John Bransby, Poe would study Latin and French but would also receive instruction in music, dancing, and drawing.

Two decades later, he would set his doppelgänger tale "William Wilson" (1839) at the Manor House School, even referring to Bransby by name; and, although there is no evidence that the story is autobiographical in other respects, its thematic focus on the instability of identity and self-knowledge may be grounded in Poe's childhood rootlessness. His fictional description of the school building bears no physical resemblance to the actual Manor House School, but the structure may reflect young Edgar's psychological alienation:

> There was really no end to its windings—to its incomprehensible subdivisions. It was difficult, at any given time, to say with certainty upon which of its two stories one happened to be. From each room to every other there were sure to be found three or four steps either in ascent or descent. Then the lateral branches were innumerable—inconceivable—and so returning in upon themselves, that our most exact ideas in regard to the whole mansion were not very far different from those with which we pondered upon infinity. During the five years of my residence here, I was never able to ascertain with precision, in what remote locality lay the little sleeping apartment assigned to myself and some eighteen or twenty other scholars. (T 1:429)

"William Wilson" is a gothic allegory of identity formation—the hedonistic narrator repeatedly flees his double and eventually murders him, at which point the second "Wilson" proclaims, "*In me didst thou exist—and, in my death, see by this image, which is thine own, how utterly thou hast murdered thyself*" (T 1:448). Tellingly, Poe not only set the story at his old school but also gave the double/protagonist his own birthday, January 19. J. Gerald Kennedy has recently argued that the tale stems from Poe's memory of being surrounded by boys who belonged to the British upper class; in his reading, the second Wilson is the American double of the narrator Wilson, a corrupt aristocrat haunted by, and obsessed with, his likeness to the foreign commoner.[19] The story is certainly some of kind of reflection on a disorienting phase of Poe's young life, when he was old enough to contemplate his place—that is to say, his placelessness—in the world, an orphan at a boarding school in a strange, foreign city.

At least, during these years, he seems to have had the affection of his foster parents, if not a great deal of their company. Allan frequently referred to Poe fondly in his letters; for example, upon their arrival, he told his partner, Charles Ellis, "Edgar says Pa say something for me, say I was not afraid coming across the Sea" and sent "Edgars love to Rosa [Edgar's sister] and Mrs. Mackenzie." A year later he reported that "Edgar [is] thin as a rasor [sic]," and elsewhere "Edgar is growing and of course thin." In 1819, writing to his uncle William Galt: "Edgar is growing wonderfully, & enjoys a good reputation and is both able & willing to receive instruction."[20] Frances Allan must have been equally proud of Edgar, but her own health fluctuated throughout their time in London, judging from Allan's letters, which hint more at annoyance than sympathy with her complaints. In their final year on Southampton Row, the overall mood grew tense: following a financial panic in 1819, Allan's London business, built on a now rapidly declining tobacco market, was failing. Deep in debt, Allan closed the London office and returned to Richmond, where, with the help of William Galt, he began rebuilding the firm.

Back in Richmond, the less prosperous Allans lived in at least three different locations over the next five years, continuing the itinerant pattern Poe would follow for the rest of his life. For the time being, his foster parents continued to indulge Edgar and seemed determined to provide him with the best education possible. While he was enrolled at Richmond Academy, at age eleven or twelve, he produced enough poems for John Allan to ask Edgar's schoolmaster, Joseph Clarke, about publishing a volume. Clarke advised against it: Poe was already a bit conceited, he said, and "it would be very injurious to the boy to allow him to be flattered and talked about as the author of a printed book at his age." Clarke later recalled that the poems "consisted chiefly of pieces addressed to the different little girls in Richmond."[21]

If Edgar felt himself an outsider again upon returning from London, he was finding ways to compensate. Now an adolescent, he was athletic and competitive; one schoolmate remembered him years later as "a swift runner, a wonderful leaper, and what was more rare, a boxer, with some slight training."[22] One June day in 1824, a fifteen-year-old Poe took a dare and swam with two other boys against a strong current on the James River; he was the only contestant to finish the race from Mayo's Island to Warwick Bar, a distance of over six miles. According to Richmond Poe historian Chris Semtner, "If Poe had never written a single poem, he would have made Richmond history for setting the record for swimming against the current in the James River."[23] In 1835, when a story appeared in the *Southern Literary Messenger* alluding to the feat, Poe corrected the writer, who had compared his achievement to Lord Byron's swimming the Hellespont in 1810: "Any swimmer 'in the falls' in my days, would have swum the Hellespont, and thought nothing of the matter," Poe boasted in the *Messenger*'s pages.[24] A classmate of Poe's at William Burke's school in 1823–24 remembered him as "a much more advanced scholar than any of us; but there was no other class for him—that being the highest—and he had nothing to do, or but little, to keep his headship of the class," adding that "in athletic exercises he was foremost."[25] A few months after the James River swim, Poe, second-in-command of a boys' club known as the Junior Morgan Riflemen, marched in a parade accompanying the Marquis de Lafayette during his visit to Richmond as part of a US tour. The Revolutionary

War hero Lafayette, while in Baltimore, had sought out the burial place of Edgar's paternal grandfather, whom he had known during the conflict. Edgar must have known about the tribute, which likely kindled his Poe family pride.

But, even as he seemed to be hitting his stride as a scholar, swimmer, and junior rifleman, Poe became increasingly introspective and less eager to please the Allans, perhaps identifying more with his absent biological family than with the foster parents who still had not made him their legal son and heir. He had been known as Edgar Allan before the family's English sojourn, but he now went by Edgar Poe.[26] In a seemingly confessional poem he would write several years later, Poe's speaker recalls,

> being young and dipt in folly
> I fell in love with melancholy,
> And used to throw my earthly rest
> And quiet all away in jest—
> I could not love except where Death
> Had mingled his with Beauty's breath—
> Or Hymen, Time, and Destiny
> Were stalking between her and me.
> ("Introduction," 1831; P 157)

While these lines betray a certain amount of Romantic posturing, they also evoke Poe's experience of love as inextricable from loss. He was probably reminded of his mother's tragic death whenever he attended church with his foster mother; the Monumental Episcopal Church, which still stands on Broad Street, was completed in 1814 on the site of a horrific fire that destroyed Richmond's most prominent theater the day after Christmas in 1811. Eliza Poe had died a few weeks earlier, but, due to the temporal proximity of her death to the larger tragedy and the fact that she had performed frequently at the Richmond Theatre, Poe—and per-

haps anyone who had known her—would likely have con-
flated her death with the fire. Seventy-two Richmonders
perished in the blaze; in fact, had John and Frances Allan
not spent the Christmas holidays, with Edgar, at a plantation on Turkey Island, east of Richmond, they likely would
have attended the theater that night themselves.[27] Public
mourning lasted months, during which theatrical performances were banned throughout the city.[28] US chief justice
John Marshall chaired the committee that decided on a
church as the most suitable memorial to the victims, who
were buried in a crypt beneath the building; construction of
Robert Mills's design, featuring an octagonal nave with a
domed cupola centered above it, began less than a year
after the fire. A receipt from December 1822 shows that the
Allans rented Pew no. 80; a plaque on the pew today names
only Frances, probably because John Allan rarely if ever attended services.[29] Marshall himself rented a pew, so it is
likely that Poe had opportunities to meet Richmond's most
prominent citizen.[30]

An angst-ridden teenager haunted by his mother's death,
Poe became infatuated with another beautiful woman he
would soon be mourning: Jane Stith Stanard, the thirty-
year-old mother of his friend Robert Craig Stanard. The
Stanard family resided just across Capitol Square from the
Allans, who were now living at Fourteenth and "Tobacco
Alley," not far from their pre-London home. Edgar spent
considerable time with the Stanards, basking in the presence
of a physically attractive, sensitive, but mentally ill woman
who died tragically the same year that Poe marched alongside Lafayette and made his famous swim. Jane Stanard's
death hit Edgar hard, and he frequently visited her grave at
the recently established municipal cemetery at Shockoe Hill,
about a mile north of downtown Richmond. He would later
claim that one of his first great poems, "To Helen" (1831),

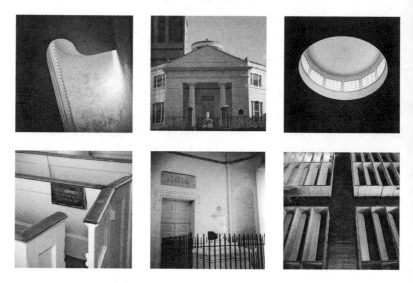

Figure 1.3 The Monumental Church, Richmond, Virginia, built on the site of the Richmond Theatre, which was destroyed by fire a few weeks after Poe's mother, an actress, died in Richmond. As a boy, Poe attended services here with his foster mother, Frances Allan.

was inspired by her. In the poem, Helen's beauty provides artistic passion, but its real purpose is to guide the speaker home:

> Helen, thy beauty is to me
>   Like those Nicéan barks of yore,
> That gently, o'er a perfumed sea,
>   The weary, way-worn wanderer bore
> To his own native shore.
>
> On desperate seas long wont to roam,
>   Thy hyancinth hair, thy classic face,
> Thy Naiad airs have brought me home
>   To the glory that was Greece,
>   And the grandeur that was Rome. (P 165–66)

If we read this poem autobiographically, Poe returns "home" not to Richmond, Virginia, and not even to a real Helen, but to an ideal of beauty that he associates with ancient Greece and Rome. Without a physical home, this wanderer seeks the comforts of art and of romantic longing itself; in the third and final stanza, he even compares Helen to a statue:

> Lo! in yon brilliant window-niche
> > How statue-like I see thee stand,
> The agate lamp within thy hand!
> > Ah, Psyche, from the regions which
> Are Holy-Land! (P 166)

Shockoe Hill Cemetery might have been this "Holy-Land," this place of inspiration, for Poe, especially when Frances Allan, who died of tuberculosis in 1829, was laid to rest there, not far from Jane Stanard. By that time, at the age of twenty, Poe would mourn his biological mother and two surrogate mothers. Eliza's grave in St. John's Churchyard, on the other side of town, was unmarked, but in Richmond he would not lack physical reminders of her, or of the other women whose affection had nourished him.

Amid the emotional turmoil of Mrs. Stanard's death and an emerging sense of independence, the rebellious teenager's relationship with his foster father was increasingly strained. Allan complained about Edgar in a letter to Edgar's brother Henry: "He does nothing & seems quite miserable, sulky & ill-tempered to all the Family. . . . The boy possesses not a Spark of affection for us nor a particle of gratitude for all my care and kindness towards him."[31] Allan had in fact supported Edgar financially as if he were his own son, but he still had not adopted him, and he was unprepared for the moodiness and spite that became Poe's defining

Figure 1.4 Jane Stith Stanard's grave in Shockoe Hill Cemetery. Stanard, the mother of one of Poe's friends, inspired the poem "To Helen."

traits during adolescence. This unfortunate turn in their relationship coincided with a sudden, though not unexpected, change in Allan's fortune. When his uncle William Galt died in 1825, Allan received a substantial inheritance. The maintenance of his foster son would now be a relatively insignificant expense, and yet with his new wealth he was less generous toward him. The awkwardness of Poe's situation became even more pronounced, for, while he shared the luxury the household now enjoyed, he was still not legally a member of the family, and the question of his own eventual

Figure 1.5 Archival photograph of the Allan mansion, Moldavia, early twentieth century, blended with a recent photograph of the site where it stood, at Fifth and Main Streets, Richmond, Virginia. John Allan purchased the house shortly after he received an enormous inheritance from his uncle William Galt in 1825. Poe lived here briefly before and after attending the University of Virginia. (Archival photograph courtesy of the Edgar Allan Poe Museum, Richmond, Virginia.)

inheritance hung in the balance of his unstable relationship with John Allan.

The Allans' newly acquired wealth was symbolized by their purchase of Moldavia, a mansion located on the southeast corner of Fifth and Main Streets, within easy walking distance of the Capitol and the center of business, but in a less crowded neighborhood, on a large parcel with eight outbuildings, gardens, and grapevines, overlooking the James River.[32] The ostentatious house was a symbol of both wealth and aristocracy: its original owners were David and Mary Randolph, members of Virginia's most prominent political family and cousins of Thomas Jefferson and John Marshall.[33]

Allan's inheritance also included three landed estates totaling more than five thousand acres, as well as several hundred slaves. Edgar probably had little firsthand experience with the large-scale plantation slavery that his foster father now directly profited from, but already he had grown up in one of the centers of the US slave trade. As Richmond merchants, John Allan and Charles Ellis could not have avoided involvement in the slave trade, and there is no indication that they wanted to: they not only bought and sold slaves but exported slave-cultivated tobacco and sold agricultural tools to plantation owners.[34] Just before leaving for England, Allan had directed his partner to sell a man named Scipio for six hundred dollars and to hire out an indeterminate number of others for fifty dollars each.[35] But as of 1825 Allan was much more deeply invested in the institution of slavery as a plantation owner, and his opulent new mansion was maintained by numerous enslaved people.

Poe encountered slavery not only as a member of a slave-owning household but also through daily exposure to enslaved factory workers—a common arrangement in antebellum Richmond—and to slave auctions. The Richmond slave trade was concentrated in the area between the James River and Broad Street, just to the south and east of the state capitol grounds, the very district where Poe lived as a boy and where his foster father worked. This slave-trade infrastructure included mainly hotels, jails, and auction houses. Hiring out, in which an owner sold a slave's labor to someone else, was standard practice for factory labor, as was "living apart"—that is, apart from owners, with cash payments to slaves, out of which owners were paid. While hired-out slaves usually experienced a degree of personal autonomy unknown to enslaved people toiling on plantations, their labor was of course still being stolen; moreover, the existential threat of being sold down the river was on constant display in the area around Fifteenth and East Main Streets. As historians Marie Tyler-McGraw and Gregg Kimball describe it, "Aside from the chains and manacles and the treatment of slaves as livestock, there was also the daily heartbreak of family separation on view. These vivid and wrenching scenes made an indelible impression on all blacks in Richmond."[36] The jails and auctions surely had a terrorizing effect, as local slaves and free blacks would have known what was described for northern white readers in contemporary slave narratives. For instance, Henry Watson, who was sold in a Richmond slave auction at age eight, offers this description of a Richmond slave trader's cruel treatment of his captives:

> If they displeased him in the least, he would order them to be stripped and tied hand and foot together. He would then have his paddle brought, which was a board about two feet in length and one inch in thickness, having fourteen holes bored through it, about an inch in circumference. This instrument of torture he would apply, until the slave was exhausted, on parts which the purchaser would not be likely to examine. This mode of punishment is considered one of the most cruel ever invented, as the flesh protrudes through these holes at every blow, and forms bunches and blisters the size of each hole, causing much lameness and soreness to the person receiving them. This punishment is generally inflicted in the morning, before visitors come to examine the slaves.[37]

Poe may not have set foot inside a slave pen or witnessed such a beating with his own eyes, but living within a few city blocks of slave jails and auction houses, he must have been well aware of the brutality that virtually surrounded him. And how might he—and, eventually, his writing—have been affected by that knowledge?

Poe undoubtedly absorbed the racism that was inextricable from slavery, and it surfaces in his depictions of African American characters in "The Man That Was Used Up," "A Predicament," and "The Gold-Bug." As an adult, he made few direct references to slavery in print, other than occasionally disparaging abolition along with everything else he associated with New England (see chapter 4). At the same time, his awareness of the arbitrary, often sadistic use of power, and the impulse to revenge, is evident in stories such as "The Cask of Amontillado," in which one man delights in chaining another man to a wall, entombing him there to perish from hunger and thirst. In other, more racially charged fictions, the tables are turned on the oppressors, with extreme vengeance: "Hop-Frog" is a thinly veiled story of slave revolt in which an abused servant, a jester "from some barbarous region . . . that no person ever heard of," convinces an evil king and his courtiers to attend a masked ball in the suggestive costume of chained orangutans, then manages to hoist them to the ceiling with a chandelier pulley and set them on fire. In the final chapters of *The Narrative of Arthur Gordon Pym*, white colonizers are entrapped by black "savages," who lead them into a narrow canyon and trigger an avalanche, burying them beneath the rubble. Although he never expressed opposition to slavery, Poe seemed acutely aware of the brutal terms on which the "peculiar institution" was maintained—and, like many other Virginians (especially after Nat Turner's 1831 rebellion in Southampton), he could envision an equally brutal uprising.

More broadly, the idea of violence perpetrated against victims who are unable to fight back—human bodies debased, subjected to torture, or treated like objects—must have made a deep impression on Poe, as such scenes pervade his fiction. Here's a partial list: in "The Fall of the House of Usher" a woman is buried alive. In "Berenice," a woman's teeth are extracted without anesthesia and she is buried alive. In "The Murders in the Rue Morgue" two women are torn apart by an orangutan: one has her throat slashed before being thrown from a fourth-story window, and the other's body is stuffed into a chimney. In "A Predicament," a woman's head is cut off. The titular character in "The Man That Was Used Up" has been completely dismembered before the story begins. Toby Dammitt in "Never Bet the Devil Your Head" is decapitated and his body is sold for dogs' meat. The narrator of "The Pit and the Pendulum" is imprisoned in a dark cell, later tied down, physically and psychologically tortured, and bitten by rats. The old man in "The Tell-Tale Heart" is suffocated, then dismembered. The wife in "The Black Cat" is murdered with an axe. In "Thou Art the Man," Barnabas Shuttleworthy is killed by a blow to the head with a rifle butt, after his horse is shot. Mistaken for a corpse, the narrator of "A Decided Loss" is subject to repeated bodily defilements before being buried alive. In some cases, Poe, or his narrator, presents this extreme physical abuse as horrific, but more often the depiction of violence shows indifference toward the suffering of the victim (as in "The Black Cat" or "The Cask of Amontillado") or is presented comically (as in "A Predicament," "Never Bet the Devil Your Head," and "Loss of Breath"). Of course, there's no single source in Poe's lived experience for the cold-blooded brutality in his stories, and there was plenty of psychotic violence in antebellum popular culture from which he could draw. And yet, growing up and later working alongside the pens, jails, and auction houses where human bodies were prepared for sale and routinely abused if the transaction did not go well, Poe must have either witnessed what survivors like Henry Watson describe, overheard them, or at the very least been aware of this facet of everyday life in his neighborhood. While Poe seeks purity, beauty, and transcendence in much of his poetry, in his fiction he seems fascinated by violence but rarely creates characters who demonstrate empathy for others or evoke it from readers. More often, his characters, like the slave trader in Henry Watson's narrative, exhibit dispassionate disregard for human dignity and the pain of others.

In February 1826, Poe enrolled at Thomas Jefferson's University of Virginia in Charlottesville, less than a year after its first classes were held. Located seventy miles northwest of Richmond in the foothills of the Blue Ridge Mountains, Charlottesville was the most secluded, rural place Poe had lived. Jefferson envisioned a community of scholars hungry for a broader education than most American colleges offered at the time, as the curriculum embraced a wider variety of natural sciences and philosophy, and, unlike other schools, it was strictly nondenominational. In that sense, it was probably a good match for the intellectually curious and not especially God-fearing Poe. In its first years, though, the university had trouble living up to Jefferson's ideals. Poe's Greek and Latin professor George Long later recalled, "The beginning of the University of Virginia was very bad. There were some excellent young men, and some of the worst that ever I knew."[38] He knew whereof he spoke: during one rampage that year, students hurled bricks and other projectiles at professors, including a bottle of urine that sailed through Professor Long's window.[39]

While Poe performed well academically—he studied ancient and modern languages exclusively—he seems, once again, to have felt out of place, surrounded by wealthy hooligans whose penchant for gambling, drinking, and brawling he found somewhat shocking. The two extant letters from Poe while at the University, both to John Allan, are dominated by references to violence, another likely source for the extreme physical cruelty in the fiction he would later write. He provided this description of one student biting another in a fight: "I saw the whole affair—it took place before my door—Wickliffe was much the strongest but not content with that—after getting the other completely in his power, he began to bite—I saw the arm afterwards—and it was really a serious matter—It was bitten from the shoulder to the elbow—and it is likely that pieces of flesh as large as my hand will be obliged to be cut out" (L 1:8–9).

While he seems to have been troubled (and fascinated) by the violence, Poe acclimated to the drinking and gambling. One classmate later recalled, rather melodramatically, "To calm & quiet the excessive nervous excitability under which he labored, he would too often put himself under the influence of that 'Invisible Spirit of Wine' which the great Dramatist has said 'If known by no other names should be called the Devil.'" Another classmate was more specific: "Poe's passion for strong drink was as marked and as peculiar as that for cards. It was not the taste of the beverage that influenced him; without a sip or smack of his mouth he would seize a full glass, without water or sugar, and send it home in a single gulp. This frequently used him up; but if not, he rarely returned to the charge."[40] If Poe hadn't known already, at the university he must have realized that he had an unhealthy relationship with alcohol, a tendency to drink quickly and excessively, and to be "used up" by it. People who knew him at various stages of his adult life described him as either abstaining from alcohol altogether, sometimes for long periods of time, or else drinking compulsively; there was no middle ground.

However, it was not the drinking but the gambling that cut short his education in Charlottesville and led to the decisive, if not final, break with Allan. Perhaps because Allan, who had not benefited from a university education himself, was skeptical or jealous of the liberal education Poe was receiving—and perhaps because the object of his charity had become sullen and ungrateful, fueling Allan's resentment—he sent his foster son to college with a very limited supply of cash. Poe would later insist that Allan had given him less than one-third of the amount required to cover his expenses, though he was, no doubt, comparing his situation to that of his free-spending classmates (L 1:59–60). Poe's questionable solution to this financial problem was to take up gambling, which resulted in debts totaling over two thousand dollars, roughly equivalent to fifty thousand dollars today.[41] Outraged, and pressed by Poe's creditors, Allan cut him off, and Poe did not return to the university in 1827.

Adding to Poe's bad luck and disillusionment was yet another loss, this one of a young woman, in a thwarted love affair. Before his departure for Charlottesville, Edgar had courted fifteen-year-old Elmira Royster; their meeting place was a spacious urban garden owned by Charles Ellis.[42] According to Elmira (in an interview long after the fact), she and Edgar had quietly become engaged before his departure for Charlottesville, but her father objected to the relationship and intercepted Poe's letters to her while he was at school, leading her to believe that Poe had lost interest in her. Though she claimed that her father had blocked her prospective union with Poe "because we were too young—no other reason," it is hard not to imagine that Mr. Royster would have been more receptive had Poe been the heir apparent to Allan's fortune. As the two families were well acquainted, Elmira's parents probably knew that he was not.[43] Two years later she married Alexander Shelton, a businessman from a wealthy family. The story of Edgar and Elmira's star-crossed love affair must have been grist for the gossip mill among the Richmond elite. Within months, the incident also made it into print—in thinly veiled, fictional form—in nearby Baltimore, as the basis for a prose tale, "The Pirate," by Poe's brother Henry, and a verse drama, *Merlin*, by Henry's friend (and later Edgar's) Lambert Wilmer.[44]

Now eighteen years old, Poe had determined to strike out on his own. Having lost Elmira and his place at the university, and having strained his relationship with his foster father to the breaking point, his comfortable life at Moldavia became deeply uncomfortable. What could he expect now from John Allan, who, on one hand, had provided him with a fine education and, for most of his childhood, had been an indulgent parent, but who, on the other hand, judged Poe harshly for his mistakes and seemed determined to cut him off financially? The push and pull between defiance and pleas for affection (and cash) in his letters to Allan is striking and at times heart-wrenching. "This is not a hurried determination," he assures Allan, "but one on which I have long considered—and having so considered[,] my resolution is unalterable—You may perhaps think that I have flown off in a passion, & that I am already wishing to return; But not so—I will give you the reasons which have actuated me, and then judge" (L 1:10). Echoing the Declaration of Independence, whose principal author had founded the school Poe had just left, Poe declared the causes that impelled him to separation.[45] He charged Allan with refusing to pay for his education ("you have blasted my hope") or to establish him in a profession. But he dug deeper, complaining that Allan simply didn't love him: "I have heard you say (when you little thought I was listening and therefore must have said it in earnest) that you had no affection for me." And, as a result, according to Poe, Allan did not treat him like a son. Poe implicitly compared his precarious position in the household to the slaves who surrounded him: "You suffer me to be subjected to the whims & caprice, not only of your white family, but the complete authority of the blacks—these grievances I could not submit to; and I am gone" (L 1:10–11).

Against his anger and sadness, Poe struggled to maintain the grown-up, legalistic language of a formal resolution. That tension continued as he asked the man he had just upbraided to send him his trunk and enough money for him to relocate and maintain himself for a month. He concluded, "If you fail to comply with my request—I tremble for the consequence" (L 1:11). Again, Poe was simultaneously issuing ultimatums and crying for affection, clearly wanting not only money but a continuation of his relationship with Allan, even as he insisted that he was breaking ties and striking out on his own. He wrote again the next day, still in Richmond, conjuring images of himself without food, wandering the streets, and promising, "I sail on Saturday." The final line before his signature was "Give my love to all at home"; the postscript read, "I have not one cent in the world to provide any food" (L 1:13).

For all the melodrama of these letters, there is no doubt that Poe was really suffering in the spring of 1827; this departure truly uprooted him and began his adult life of itinerancy. That is not to say that the break with Allan was clean—they later reconciled and split again, and the trail of letters continued for another six years. But Edgar would return to the events that precipitated his flight from Richmond in 1827 in those later letters, repeatedly trying to justify his actions in Charlottesville, regain Allan's affection, and, of course, convince him to send money. Also, in those letters, he would repeatedly use the word "home" in reference to Richmond and Moldavia. In February 1829, trying to explain to Allan what went wrong two years earlier, Poe would write, "I had never been from home before for any

length of time" (L 1:20). In July 1829, writing from Baltimore upon receiving some money from Allan, he refers to
"the length of time I have been from home," and, sadly,
writes asking "for information as to what course I must pursue—I would have returned home immediately but for the
words [in] your letter 'I am not particularly anxious to see
you'—I know not how to interpret them" (L 1:37–38).

The years following Poe's departure would see more false
starts and changes of direction and habitation. As described
in the next chapter, his quest for a literary career would
eventually bring him back to Richmond several years later,
for just over a year, as he sought to build on his initial success as a writer in Baltimore. But in March 1827, the
eighteen-year-old really had little choice but to leave Richmond and John Allan. Staying would have been humiliating, and although he was far from attaining financial independence in 1827, he had to try. The city had been a kind of
anchor for a young man whose childhood—particularly
early childhood—had been profoundly unsettled, yet he had
come to realize that the anchor was not firmly fixed, since
his place in Richmond depended on his dubious status
within the Allan family. But Poe knew that his mother Eliza
had thrived (for a while) without a hometown, and as a boy
in London he had seen something of the wide world beyond
Virginia. Eliza had left her young son a watercolor of Boston Harbor, with the inscription: "For my little son Edgar,
who should ever love Boston, the place of his birth, and
where his mother found her *best*, and *most sympathetic*
friends."[46] So perhaps it is not surprising that Edgar, feeling
more Poe than Allan, would leave the town he thought of
as home and return to the city of his birth.

CHAPTER 2

Baltimore (1827–1838)

Having declared his independence and left Richmond and John Allan—forever, he imagined—in the spring of 1827, Poe traveled by ship to Boston, the city of his birth. Over the decade that followed, he would become, as he phrased it in "To Helen," a "weary, way-worn wanderer." Accordingly, this chapter follows Poe up and down the East Coast as he repeatedly reinvented himself (as soldier, cadet, poet, satirist, critic, editor) but focuses in particular on his experience in Baltimore, where he lived briefly in 1829 and then returned, in 1831, for four years. It was not so much the length of his residence that makes Baltimore the primary focus of this chapter as it is the significance of his time there: in Baltimore, he taught himself to write fiction for magazines, and he found a family.

Edgar did not stay long in Boston in 1827, and yet he was, in a sense, reborn there, as a published poet, arranging with Calvin A. Thomas to print at most two hundred copies of a slender volume entitled *Tamerlane and Other Poems.* His first publication went almost unnoticed, and he allowed it to remain "lost" for the rest of his career. His name does not appear on the title page, which reads "by a Bostonian." An epigraph from the poet William Cowper on the same page—"Young heads are giddy, and young hearts are warm, / And make mistakes for manhood to reform"—reflects the subject matter of Poe's early poems, as well as the transitional moment in which he found himself as he temporarily reclaimed his identity as a Bostonian, shedding his Rich-

mond skin. In the long title poem, Poe's Byronic hero Tamerlane recounts his youthful quest for glory, achieved at
the cost of true love and happiness. "I reached my home—
my home no more— / For all had flown that made it so"
(P 39), he says, upon learning that the woman of his dreams
has died while he was conquering the world. Whether cast-
ing himself in the role of Tamerlane or, in other poems,
adopting a more transparently autobiographical "I," Poe
presents himself as youthful but world-weary, haunted by
his own dreams and his belief in a dark personal destiny. In
a poem titled "Dreams," Poe clings to some alternate reality, even one of "hopeless sorrow":

> 'Twere better than the dull reality
> Of waking life, to him whose heart shall be,
> And hath been ever, on the chilly earth,
> A chaos of deep passion from his birth! (P 68)

By the time *Tamerlane and Other Poems* rolled off the
press in the summer of 1827, its homeless author had enlisted in the US Army, covering his tracks by using the name
Edgar A. Perry; he was assigned to Fort Independence in
Boston Harbor. Before the end of the year, his company
shipped to Fort Moultrie on Sullivan's Island, South Carolina. While stationed there, throughout 1828, Poe must have
visited nearby Charleston, where his mother had performed
on several occasions, the last of which was in January 1811,
when he was two years old. Some traces of Poe's time in the
South Carolina Lowcountry surface in his later work. If he
explored the files of the Charleston *Courier* looking for references to his mother, he might have found an 1807 poem
entitled "The Mourner," which bears an unmistakable resemblance to "Annabel Lee," the ballad he would write
weeks before his death in 1849.[1] He would also use Sullivan's
Island as the setting of his sensational buried-treasure tale

"The Gold-Bug" in 1843 and as the landing strip for a transatlantic balloon voyage in a newspaper hoax in 1844. But, throughout his career, when asked for biographical information, Poe chose to substitute stories of foreign adventure in Greece and Russia for his more mundane service as an enlisted man, and with it his year on Sullivan's Island. Consequently, biographical articles on Poe up until the 1880s contain no references to Private Edgar Perry, and very few people who knew him as Edgar Poe (perhaps only the Allans) were aware of that chapter of his life.

While the mythical Poe whose image we carry around today—the impulsive, undisciplined, and rebellious genius—would seem ill suited for army life, he actually thrived during his two years of enlistment. As one of the few literate soldiers in his company, he was appointed company clerk while at Fort Moultrie, and was later promoted to sergeant major, the army's highest noncommissioned rank.[2] Perhaps more consistent with our contemporary, gothic image, Poe also served as an artificer, a maker of explosive devices.[3] His term of enlistment was five years, but, after less than two, he wanted out; just before his company was transferred in December 1828 to Fortress Monroe near Hampton, Virginia, he began asking his foster father to approve his discharge (a condition set by his commanding officer). Lest Allan see this request as a sign of failure or retreat, Poe again played up his ambition and independence: "I have thrown myself upon the world, like the Norman conqueror on the shores of Britain &, by my avowed assurance of victory, have destroyed the fleet which could alone cover my retreat—I must either conquer or die—succeed or be disgraced" (L 1:15). At the same time, Poe needed Allan's help, but his foster father was in no hurry to provide it; at least three letters from Poe between December and February went unanswered.

A temporary turning point in their relationship came with the death of Frances Allan, at the age of forty-four, on February 28. She had been ill for some time, possibly from tuberculosis, declining while Poe was away. No letters from Poe to his foster mother survive, and he made few references to her later in life, but he must have felt considerable tenderness and gratitude for the woman who had given him a comfortable childhood and some measure of maternal affection. Following her death, Edgar reconciled with Allan, who sanctioned the discharge and paid for a substitute to serve the rest of his enlistment term. He also supported Poe's new plan: to obtain an appointment to the US Military Academy and return to the army as an officer. Poe's West Point aspiration might have sprung from this reconciliation; he hadn't mentioned it in his earlier letters, but now that he once again felt like John Allan's son, this more conventional, gentlemanly career path seems to have replaced whatever ship-burning, world-conquering scheme he had previously imagined as a way of becoming the next Byron.

Poe had reengaged Allan's support, but relations between them still must have been too tepid for him to remain at Moldavia, the family mansion, because, after a brief stay in Richmond, he moved temporarily to Baltimore in May 1829, stopping in Washington, DC, to meet with secretary of war John Eaton about the appointment to West Point. The Poe family had deep roots in Baltimore, most auspiciously in the person of Poe's late grandfather, "General" David Poe, a merchant and wheel manufacturer who held the position of assistant deputy quartermaster general during the Revolutionary War. His widow, Elizabeth Cairnes Poe, was living there with her daughter Maria Clemm, also widowed, and Maria's two children. Edgar may have lived with them for at least part of this stay; he lodged for some (probably brief) period in Beltzhoover's Hotel at Hanover and Baltimore

Streets, the same building where Francis Scott Key had written "The Star-Spangled Banner" fifteen years earlier. In June, trying to explain to John Allan what had become of some money he had sent, he reported that his cousin, Edward Mosher, had stolen forty-six dollars from him at Beltzhoover's while they were sharing a room (L 1:33). There is no evidence of Poe working for money during this approximately six-month period; temporarily in Allan's good graces, he expected his foster father to provide for him while he petitioned for a place on the roll at West Point. Introducing himself in a letter to the novelist and editor John Neal, Poe explained that "I am and have been, from my childhood, an idler" (L 1:47). That characterization was partly the pose of a budding Romantic author, but it rings true for this stage of his life. Poe remained in Baltimore for the rest of 1829, with one brief visit to Philadelphia to try to arrange publication of a second book of poems, and another trek— literally on foot, or so he claimed—to Washington, to see Secretary Eaton again in July.

Meanwhile, having failed to persuade the Philadelphia publisher Carey, Lea & Carey, Poe arranged with a small Baltimore firm, Hatch & Dunning, to print a few hundred copies of a book titled *Al Aaraaf, Tamerlane, and Minor Poems* in December 1829. Like its predecessor, *Al Aaraaf* mined Poe's early preoccupation with dreams and youthful, romantic angst; this volume, too, was destined for obscurity, though it did receive a handful of notices in the press. Allan continued to support Poe's West Point ambition; he kept sending Edgar money through the end of 1829, and Poe in return sent him a copy of *Al Aaraaf*. Allan brought Poe back into his Richmond household in early 1830, as his name made its way up West Point's waiting list.

Not surprisingly, the rapprochement between Poe and Allan proved temporary. Poe was finally admitted to West

Point, but, before departing in May or June, he received a letter from Sergeant Samuel "Bully" Graves, who had assumed the remainder of his term of enlistment in the army: Poe still owed him money for the arrangement. In his reply, Poe placed the blame on his foster father, claiming, "Mr. A is not very often sober" (L 1:54). Determined to get paid, Graves must have revealed the contents of Poe's letter to Allan, infuriating him. Frances Allan's death the previous year had opened the door for reconciliation, but John Allan's marriage in the fall of 1830—to Louisa Patterson of New York—seems to have closed off any remaining affection he might have felt for Edgar.[4] Allan did not visit Poe at West Point while in New York for his wedding, nor was Poe invited to the ceremony; in fact, Allan made it clear that he did not wish to hear from him. Poe's response, after another long, defensive letter to Allan, was to leave West Point by way of court-martial: in January he simply stopped showing up for drills, roll calls, and class, and, on February 18, he was dismissed. Though briefer than his army stint, Poe's six months at West Point were similar in that he seemed comfortable enough with military discipline and excelled academically (finishing third in French and seventeenth in mathematics on his exams in a class of eighty-seven) until he abruptly decided to move on. The timing, coupled with Poe's correspondence with Allan, strongly suggests that his departure was prompted by Allan's marriage and severance of communication. As a practical matter, the academy did not provide living expenses, and now neither would Allan; more significant, Poe's vision of himself as an officer and gentleman dissolved, as he once again had no claim to Allan's name or fortune.

Before leaving West Point, Poe collected subscription funds from his fellow cadets for a third volume of poetry. He had written some satirical verse during his time as a cadet, and his classmates must have been eager to see some of it in print. Poe accordingly had the book printed in New York City when he left the academy, and dedicated *Poems by Edgar A. Poe, Second Edition* "To the U. S. Army Corps of Cadets." But the contents, devoid of West Point humor, probably disappointed those first readers. In fact, one cadet inscribed his copy, "This book is a damn cheat."[5] Like *Al Aaraaf*, the 1831 volume collects some of the stronger previously published verse along with new material, this "second edition" implicitly suppressing the 1827 *Tamerlane and Other Poems*. While still introspective, the new poems—including "To Helen," "Israfel," and "The Doomed City" (later retitled "The City in the Sea")—are less self-pitying and generally more mature, exhibiting a richer vocabulary and more compelling imagery than his earlier verse. The four years between his first collection and this third, between his eighteenth and twenty-second years, had been full of movement and uncertainty: Boston, Sullivan's Island, Old Point Comfort, Baltimore, Richmond, and West Point, oscillating between independence and attachment (emotional and financial) to John Allan. Now he found himself in New York, penniless and ill, so he swallowed his pride yet again and appealed to Allan for money. A few weeks later, he wrote to his former superintendent at West Point, asking for a certificate showing his high class rank prior to dismissal—that, and a personal reference letter to anyone he might know in Paris.

Poe never made it to Paris, but instead moved back to Baltimore in the spring of 1831. Though in his desperation he still regarded John Allan as a potential source of cash, there was no going back to Moldavia now, and living anywhere else in Richmond with no means of support, as well as with the stigma of being a rich man's disowned foster child, would have been unbearable. His closest family, the household headed by his father's sister Maria Clemm, was in Baltimore.

Like Richmond, Baltimore had established itself in the late eighteenth and early nineteenth centuries as a hub of regional commerce, thanks to a vibrant shipping trade and, especially as overland transportation developed, access to wheat and other crops. Also like Richmond, local manufacturing was starting to play a larger role in the city's economy by the 1820s and 1830s, as New York increasingly dominated the European import-export market. Baltimore's overseas shipping was slumping somewhat in the 1830s, but the port remained vital to the local economy, with over five hundred vessels arriving annually.[6] The young city had all but missed out on canal building as a means of connecting raw materials, manufacture, and markets, but the city took the lead in regional rail transportation: work on the Baltimore & Ohio Railroad began in 1828 with a combination of horse and steam power, and it was taking passengers soon afterward.[7] Meanwhile, new industries included copper and chemical factories as well as iron-rolling mills, while smaller manufactories were producing tinware, gunpowder, cigars, stoves, clothing, and other consumer goods.[8]

Accordingly, the city was growing rapidly: in the 1830 census, Baltimore passed Philadelphia, becoming second to New York City in population, five times the size of Richmond. Its population increased sevenfold (from 13,500 to 102,300) in the half-century from 1790 to 1840, driven by immigration; in immigrant population, too, it was second only to New York, albeit a distant second.[9] Baltimore was a young city, and it must have felt that way, with relatively few "native" residents in the 1830s mixing with thousands of recent arrivals.[10] A large portion of the populace—one-fourth as of 1820—was African American, but the number of enslaved Baltimoreans was decreasing as the free black population rose dramatically in the first half of the century.[11]

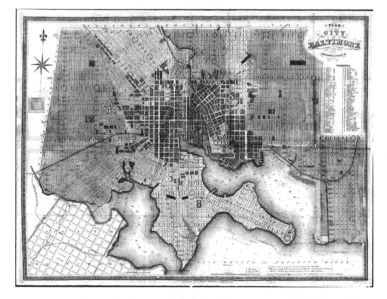

Figure 2.1 Plan of Baltimore, Maryland, in 1836, with darkened areas indicating development. Poe's residences with the Clemm family, Mechanics Row (1) and North Amity Street (2) are marked. (Courtesy of the Library of Congress, Geography and Map Division.)

Throughout this expansion, Baltimore's identity was a work in progress, less defined than other major East Coast cities. Boston was regarded as the cradle of American civilization, Puritan and Revolutionary; New York was already Gotham, the commercial and cultural heart of the nation; Philadelphia was the Quaker City, its patron saint the wise and practical Ben Franklin. Richmond, the capital not only of Virginia but of the upper south, was defined largely by its planter/merchant aristocracy. Baltimore, though, was culturally both north and south. Its economy was not dependent on slave labor but certainly made use of it; even as slavery declined there, abolition would never take hold.

Baltimore barely existed as a city prior to the Revolution, in which it played a relatively small role, but recent history, particularly the War of 1812, along with the boosterism surrounding the B&O Railroad, provided a foundation for civic pride. In 1815, the year after the Battle of Baltimore and the defense of Fort McHenry, the city commissioned Maximilien Godefroy to design the Battle Monument: placed on a centrally located square along Calvert Street between Fayette and Lexington, the neoclassical column bore the inscription "Baltimore pledges eternal remembrance to the republican virtue of her sons."[12] That same year, the cornerstone for another, much taller column in honor of George Washington was laid on a hill just north of the city. Designed by Robert Mills, architect of Richmond's Monumental Church and, later, the more famous Washington Monument, it was a highly visible landmark. These two new monuments were enough for John Quincy Adams to dub Baltimore "the Monumental City," but Godefroy, Mills, and Benjamin Henry Latrobe also designed a number of imposing neoclassical buildings (both public and private) that enhanced the cityscape's "monumental" feel. [13] The city also boasted five public fountains, set off on landscaped squares.[14] Frances Trollope, in her widely read *Domestic Manners of the Americans*, described the favorable visual impression Baltimore made in the 1830s, calling it "one of the handsomest cities to approach in the Union. The noble column erected to the memory of Washington, and Catholic Cathedral, with its beautiful dome, being built on a commanding eminence, are seen at a great distance. As you draw nearer, many other domes and towers become visible, and as you enter Baltimore-street, you feel that you are arrived in a handsome and populous city. . . . even the private dwelling-houses have a look of magnificence, from the abundance of white marble with which many of them are adorned."[15]

Like other northeastern cities, Baltimore was building local infrastructure in the form of gas pipes to provide

Figure 2.2 *View of Baltimore*, William H. Bartlett, 1840. This somewhat idealized painting conveys both the "monumental" image of the city and the encroachment of industrial smokestacks. (Reproduced with permission from Steve Bartrick Antique Prints & Maps.)

streetlights, and sixteen miles of water lines.[16] But the "internal improvements" that would bolster commerce with other regions was a greater source of pride. The cornerstone-laying ceremony for the B&O on July 4, 1828, was accompanied by a parade of representatives of various trades and manufacturers, a patriotic celebration of the bright future the railroad promised. The city's printers mounted a handpress onto a platform, from which they issued copies of the Declaration of Independence.[17] A song written for the event shows the public face of a city determined to compete with New York and Philadelphia:

> Here's a rode [*sic*] to be made,
> With the Pick and the Spade,
> 'Tis to reach to Ohio, for the benefit of trade;
> Here are mountains to be levell'd,

Here are vallies [*sic*] to be fill'd,
Here are rocks to be blown, and bridges too to build.
And we're all hopping, skipping, jumping,
And we're all crazy here in Baltimore.[18]

Of course, this official can-do, "crazy" spirit was probably not so deeply felt among the working people who made Baltimore's growth possible. As historian Seth Rockman demonstrates in his book *Scraping By*, the typical wage for a day laborer, seventy-five cents a day, could not really support a family; households were maintained by pooling meager resources—women's sewing, for instance, along with men's wage-earning and children's scavenging.[19] Women were the heads of between 10 and 20 percent of Baltimore households, such as the one Poe joined in the spring of 1831.

Managed by Maria Clemm, the family depended on income from several sources: most significantly, Poe's bedridden grandmother received a widow's pension of $240 per year, comparable to what an unskilled male laborer could earn. Maria earned additional money from needlework, and, at some point, the household included Edgar's brother, Henry, who had a serious drinking problem but was probably still capable of earning some money from day labor. The forty-one-year-old Maria was also the mother of two children: Henry, thirteen, and Virginia, nine. They lived in a two-story house, most likely occupying only the second floor, on a block of Wilks Street—now the 1000 block of Eastern Avenue between Exeter Street and Central Avenue—known as Mechanics Row. Theirs was probably the corner house on a row of eight sharing a single roofline, two-story structures with dormers and small stoops.[20] The "Hartford Run," which ran alongside their house, was in effect an open sewer.[21] Historians Mary Markey and Dean Krimmel describe this part of the Fells Point areas as "a solidly respectable middle-class neighborhood" at the time, but the Clemms' living space was undoubtedly crowded, and they were probably able to afford the rent only because of Elizabeth Cairnes Poe's annuity.[22]

According to the 1830 census, conducted the year before Edgar moved in, the Clemm household on Mechanics Row also included an enslaved African American woman.[23] She might not have been the only enslaved person to pass through Maria's ownership: a 1940 *Baltimore Sun* article claimed the discovery of a bill of sale from December 1829 for a "Negro" named Edwin, in which Edgar Poe acted as Maria's agent.[24] (The actual document has never been produced, but the scenario is hardly far-fetched.) Edwin was sold for forty dollars as a "term slave" who would be manumitted (at least in theory) nine years later at the age of thirty.[25] Maria might have purchased Edwin specifically to hire him out as a source of income, but then sold his term in exchange for a larger, one-time sum. If that were the case, she would not have been exceptional as a white Baltimorean of modest means investing in slave labor as a commodity. Like Edwin, the enslaved woman who appears on the 1830 census might have been another income source for the household (which probably could not afford to keep a "servant") or she might have been owned by someone else while boarding with the Clemms, again to provide additional income. (Of course, none of this mitigates the immorality of Maria's engagement with slavery; I am merely speculating as to why a household of such limited means would have included an enslaved person.) In any case, the woman's presence would not have been unusual; seven out of nine households on Mechanics Row in 1830 included either enslaved or free blacks.[26] With that in mind, it is entirely possible that Poe crossed paths with a teenage Frederick Bailey, a slave who was hired out to a Fells Point shipbuilder in the early 1830s, and who would soon escape to New York and take the name of Frederick Douglass.[27]

While living on Mechanics Row, Poe seems to have contributed very little to the family coffers, though documentation of his activities during the early 1830s is so scarce that it is hard to be sure. He had little inclination to seek the kind of manual day labor that was building up the city in these years; some combination of class-consciousness and faith in his calling as an author probably prevented it. Indeed, despite his having been an athletic teenager and having met the physical demands of the army and West Point, it is hard to imagine Poe working in a factory, sweeping chimneys, or toiling on the "mud machine" that continually dredged the silt from Baltimore harbor.

It is unclear exactly how long Poe's older brother lived with Maria Clemm and her family, but Henry and Edgar were both members of the household in the spring and summer of 1831. They had not lived together since their mother died, but they had seen each other and corresponded over the years and apparently felt a strong mutual attachment. The overseas travel that Edgar would fabricate in his own biography was borrowed from Henry's real life in either the navy or merchant marine. Henry, too, was a writer; in fact, a few of Edgar's early verses are virtually identical to poetry published under Henry's name, leaving open the question of which brother actually wrote them.[28] The circumstances surrounding their reunion were tragic, however; at the age of twenty-four, Henry had fallen victim to alcoholism and tuberculosis. When he died on August 1, 1831, the funeral service was held in the house on Mechanics Row. A few years later, in tribute to his brother, Poe would have his fictional character Augustus Barnard, the adventurous bosom friend of his novel's narrator, Arthur Gordon Pym (whose name echoes its author's), die at sea on August 1.

In October 1831, about half a year after moving to Baltimore, Edgar briefly resumed his correspondence with John Allan, making a familiar request for money, which Allan apparently provided. A month later, Poe reported to Allan that he was in jail, "arrested eleven days ago [November 7, 1831] for a debt which I never expected to have to pay, and which was incurred as much on H[enr]y's account as on my own about two years ago" (L 1:69). Imprisonment for debt was not unusual: it happened to over nine hundred Baltimoreans in 1831, and for less than ten-dollar debts in half those cases.[29] Poe asked Allan for eighty dollars; then his aunt Maria followed up, begging Allan for help in "extricating" his foster son. Poe wrote Allan yet again on December 15, and again two weeks after that. Allan eventually aided Poe one last time, but his help did not arrive until mid-January; according to Allan's own note on one of Poe's letters, he wrote to an associate in Baltimore to "procure his liberation" in December but "neglected" to send the instructions for over a month.[30] Allan never wrote to Poe again. He did scribble on one of Poe's old letters, referring to its author's "Blackest Heart & deepest ingratitude," and prophesizing that "his Talents are of an order that can never prove a comfort to their possessor."[31] Poe would make just one more appeal to Allan a little over a year later and, having heard that Allan was seriously ill, may have tried to visit him at Moldavia in early 1834. It probably came as no surprise that when Allan died that March, he made no mention of his foster son in his will.

Up until his move to Baltimore, Poe had imagined himself strictly a poet: had he been John Allan's heir, he could have been a gentlemanly "man of letters" or a rebellious—but still affluent—American Byron. But now, out of economic necessity, he had come to see writing as a profession, in the sense that he would produce texts for an impersonal market of readers and, one would hope, make a living at it. This obviously was not happening with his books of poetry, so Poe turned to the seemingly more marketable genre of prose fiction. In January 1832, perhaps while he was still in jail, he published his first story, "Metzengerstein," in a Philadelphia paper called the *Saturday Courier*. The *Courier* had advertised a contest, soliciting original tales with a prize of one hundred dollars (probably a year's rent for the Clemm household) going to the writer whose work was judged best by the editors. Literary competitions of this type were common throughout antebellum America. They were a gamble for authors, who would receive a large payment if they won but nothing if they lost, while the sponsoring periodical would acquire the right to publish, for free, any or all submissions.[32] Looking to increase his odds, Poe sent five stories, none of which was deemed equal to "Love's Martyr" by Delia S. Bacon. After "Metzengerstein," a gothic revenge tale, the *Courier* would eventually publish the rest of Poe's entries—"The Duc de l'Omelette," "A Tale of Jerusalem," "A Decided Loss," and "Bon-Bon," all satires—but he would receive no payment; his name would not even appear as the author of the other four stories. Such was Poe's introduction to the world he would later call the "magazine prison-house."

Despite not getting paid for these first five tales, Poe realized that entering competitions was a fairly sensible strategy for an unknown writer delving into a new genre. And although Baltimore was not on a par with New York or Philadelphia as a publishing center, it was a striving city eager to compete with its northern neighbors, and therefore not a bad place to (re)launch a literary career. Magazines and newspapers proliferated there; by one count, Baltimore produced seventy-eight periodicals between 1815 and 1833, although many of them were short-lived.[33] More than twenty bookstores, some of which doubled as publishers, opened their doors during the same period, clustered along Baltimore Street, the central east-west corridor. The city also supported five subscription libraries, most notably the Baltimore Library Company, which allowed nonsubscribers like Poe to read its volumes on site, and several theaters offering a range of productions including Shakespeare, light opera, and contemporary melodramas.[34] At the same time, literary Baltimore was a small enough world that Poe could become quickly recognized. Even during his brief residence there in 1829, by publishing *Al Aaraaf, Tamerlane, and Minor Poems*, Poe gained some local attention. One episode, generally credited by scholars, has Poe losing a speed-writing bet at Seven Swans Tavern with a doctor-poet named John Lofland, the "Milford Bard," over who could crank out more stanzas in an hour.[35] The 1830 verse satire "The Musiad, or Ninead" pokes fun at writers from Baltimore and Philadelphia; Poe is gently teased but also praised for his precociousness throughout ten of the poem's 101 lines: "Next Poe who smil'd at reason, laugh'd at law, / And played a tune who should have played at taw [marbles], / Now strain'd a license, and now crack'd a string, / But sang as other children dare not sing."[36]

The roll call of regional poets in "The Musiad" suggests that literary Baltimore was a small world, in which a newcomer like Poe would be noticed. Like other cities, Baltimore was home to at least a few literary organizations that allowed for networking while maintaining a somewhat insular environment. The most prominent of these, the Delphian Club, had disbanded by the 1830s, but it would have been part of local lore, which Poe certainly would have absorbed. Drawing upon the practices of eighteenth-century literary coteries, the Delphian Club was exclusive, made up of writers who shared their work with each other and adopted comical pseudonyms such as Solomon Fitz-Quizz and Jehu O'Cataract. One Delphian, William Gwynn, was among Poe's best-placed contacts when he moved to the city: Gwynn had known Edgar's father David and, more recently, had employed Edgar's second cousin Neilson Poe. Edgar had sent the manuscript of his second collection to Gwynn in 1829, seeking his help in getting it published, and he appealed (unsuccessfully) to Gwynn for a job with his *Federal Gazette and Baltimore Daily Advertiser* upon moving back in 1831.[37]

Poe almost certainly had this kind of club in mind as he constructed a fictional frame for a collection of stories he would call *Tales of the Folio Club*.[38] Adding six new stories to the five published in the *Saturday Courier*, he assigned each one to a comically named author (Solomon Seadrift, Mr. Rouge-et-Noir) and presented the collection as a set of manuscripts seized from a meeting of the club. Poe's fictional stand-in, outraged at having his own story judged the worst, absconds with the evening's offerings and has them published to embarrass the group, which he calls a "Junto of *Dunderheadism*" (T 1:203). Although the collection would never be published as such, the concept highlights Poe's ambitions and expectations in the early 1830s. For one thing, he was still thinking in terms of books (in this case, a collection of tales) even as he was experimenting with a form whose primary medium was the magazine. Moreover, he wanted to demonstrate his versatility: each Folio Club tale was supposed to have been written by a separate author, but all of them—tales and authors—were clearly Poe's creations. Finally, he sought to position himself as both insider (he knows how these literary clubs operate) and outsider (he is insulted by them and mocks them). It is a model for the relationship to the publishing establishment that Poe would claim throughout his career.

But Poe hadn't given up on poetry entirely, and, in early 1833, he began publishing poems in a Baltimore weekly, the *Saturday Visiter*. That summer, when the *Visiter* advertised another contest with cash prizes of fifty dollars for fiction and twenty-five dollars for poetry, he sent all six of his new "Folio Club" tales as well as the poem "The Coliseum." The three judges were impressed; when they announced the winners in October 1833, they made it clear their task amounted to choosing which of Poe's tales should win the fiction prize. They wisely chose "MS. Found in a Bottle," Poe's most immersive and provocative early story. The judges were also taken with Poe's poem, a rather conventional tribute to the famous Roman ruin, but awarded that prize to "The Song of the Winds" by one Henry Wilton. When Poe heard that he had been denied the poetry prize because he had already secured the honors for fiction, and—even worse—that "Wilton" was actually John H. Hewitt, the editor of the *Saturday Visiter*, he was outraged, and confronted Hewitt, who later claimed to have "dealt [Poe] a blow which staggered him, for I was physically his superior."[39]

"Of my country and of my family I have little to say. Ill usage and length of years have driven me from the one, and estranged me from the other": so begins Poe's prize-winning "MS. Found in a Bottle." These sentiments reflect not just the "ill usage" he certainly felt at the hands of John Allan but the general estrangement he experienced during these pivotal years. Of course, the narrator is not Poe; in fact, at the outset of his adventure he is, in one important sense, Poe's opposite: "I have often been reproached with the aridity of my genius; a deficiency of imagination has been imputed to me as a crime" (T 1:135). In other words, this is not the hyperimaginative, haunted speaker of Poe's early poetry—not yet, anyway. As a passenger on a voyage to the Malay Archipelago, he encounters a seemingly supernatural

Figure 2.3 The October 19, 1833, issue of the *Saturday Visiter* included Henry Wilton's (John Hewitt's) prize poem "Song of the Winds" (left column) and Poe's prize story "MS. Found in a Bottle."

storm, which eventually hurls his ship into "some watery hell," specifically a giant whirlpool, where it is destroyed by another, much larger vessel, onto which the writer miraculously lands. Gradually, he deduces that he has boarded a ghost ship, like the Flying Dutchman, and that he has crossed over to a liminal afterlife: "We are surely doomed to hover continually upon the brink of eternity, without taking a final plunge into the abyss" (T 1:143). Before the "manuscript" breaks off, he conjectures that "we are hurrying onwards to some exciting knowledge—some never-to-be-imparted secret, whose attainment is destruction" (T 1:145).

"MS. Found in a Bottle" is thus a parable of a quickening imagination—appropriate for a young man discovering his powers as a fiction writer—and a speculation on postmortem consciousness. It should come as no surprise that Poe, who had recently lost his brother and was still no doubt haunted by earlier deaths—Helen Stanard, Frances Allan, and, most significant, his mother—would turn repeatedly to scenarios in which death is not the end. But, keeping in mind the tale's opening sentences, we might also see it as a reflection of Poe's own marginal existence. A year earlier, alone in New York, he had described his condition to Allan as delirious and near death: "I have no money—no friends—I have written to my brother—but he cannot help me—I shall never rise from my bed—besides a most violent cold on my lungs my *ear* discharges blood and matter continuall[y] and my headache is distracting—I hardly know what I am writing" (L 1:64). More recently, he had been jailed for debt. And, until this very story won its prize, he was a professed writer who had made no money whatsoever from his publications, and who was dependent on the generosity of relatives. Like that ship, Poe was living on the edge; like his narrator, he was writing for an audience that might never find him.

Poe wasn't writing directly about Baltimore, but the anxieties he was experiencing there—particularly the possibility that, like Henry, he could die young (and what then?)—surface in these early imitations and satires. In various ways, the dead return or remain alive in the tales from the early 1830s: in his first published story, "Metzengerstein," a murdered nobleman reappears as a horse to carry off his nemesis; in the comic "Duc de l'Omelette," the effete title character successfully cheats in a card game with the Devil to preserve his soul. In "The Assignation," two lovers carry out a suicide pact in order to be together for eternity. "Shadow.—A Parable" begins, "Ye who read are still among the living; but I who write shall have long since gone my way into the region of shadows" (T 1:188).[40]

His most trenchant early comic story, "A Decided Loss," not only straddles the line between living and dead but also dramatizes the indignities of urban life, where an anonymous human body is completely depersonalized. As the story begins, the narrator is yelling at his wife, until he discovers that he can no longer speak, or exhale, because he has literally lost his breath. He is therefore taken for dead, a scenario that leads to his being abused—violently, repeatedly—for comic effect. Crushed by passengers on a mail stage, he is thrown out of the coach; while awaiting burial, his nose is chewed off by a couple of cats. He escapes from that predicament only to be mistaken for a condemned criminal and hanged; in the deliberately absurd logic of the tale, he can't defend himself because he can't speak, but neither can he perish on the gallows, having already lost his breath. Purchased by a physician for twenty-five dollars, his body is subjected to dissection and experimentation: his tormentor attributes his "kicking and plunging" (in an effort to prove "my existence") to the electric charge of a galvanic battery. The story's humor is grotesque and cartoonish, but underneath the slapstick is a man who has become an object, stripped of his dignity, unsure whether he's dead or alive.

Another story added to the Folio Club lineup, "King Pest," is set during the Black Plague in the fourteenth century, but its more immediate inspiration was probably the cholera pandemic of 1832, which struck Baltimore as well as other northeastern cities.[41] A pair of seaman exploring a disease-ravaged London discover a macabre, drunken gathering presided over by the dead-alive figures of King and Queen Pest: drinking toasts to Death in a chamber decorated with skeletons, the assembled "royalty" (the Arch Duke Pest-Iferous, the Duke Tem-Pest, the Arch Duchess Ana-Pest) are both victims and personifications of pestilence. This grotesque dark comedy is yet another instance of Poe's preoccupation, from the beginning of his career as a fiction writer, with a basic, inescapable question—what is it like to be dead?—something he must have contemplated often during these desperate years.

In addition to providing much-needed income, the *Saturday Visiter* contest introduced Poe to one of its judges, who proved to be a valuable mentor: John Pendleton Kennedy, a former Delphian Club member, one of Baltimore's most prominent writers (he had recently published a popular novel, *Swallow Barn*) and one of its leading citizens. In a November 1834 letter, Poe provided Kennedy with an abridged (and not entirely accurate) version of his relationship with John Allan, ending with what he now described as a disinheritance: "I am thrown entirely upon my own resources with no profession, and very few friends. Worse than all this, I am at length penniless" (L 1:79). The following year, when Kennedy invited Poe to dinner, Poe replied by requesting a loan of twenty dollars so that he could buy clothes decent enough to make himself presentable. Kennedy later reported, "I gave him clothing, free access to my table and the use of a horse for exercise whenever he chose; in fact brought him up from the very verge of despair" (L 1:83). Kennedy tried to help Poe with his Folio Club volume, sending the manuscript to the publishing firm of Carey & Lea. Probably out of deference to Kennedy, Henry Carey said he would publish Poe's book, even though "I do not expect to make anything." Meanwhile, Carey advised Poe (via Kennedy) to sell his stories to magazines and gift books, though virtually all of them had already appeared in either the *Saturday Courier* or the *Visiter*.[42] Carey stalled when Kennedy followed up on Poe's behalf, and "Tales of the Folio Club" was never published.

While living on Mechanics Row, Poe became romantically involved with a woman from the neighborhood named

Mary Starr, also known as Mary Devereaux. She was about seventeen at the time, about five years younger than Edgar. Because Starr gave her account of the relationship over fifty years after the fact, there is reason to question the accuracy of her details, but she provided an unusually vivid portrait of Poe during a period for which there is little other biographical evidence. She described him as passionate, impulsive, and jealous, suggesting that being Poe's girlfriend was a tough job:

> My intimacy with Mr. Poe isolated me a good deal. In fact my girl friends were many of them afraid of him, and forsook me on that account. I knew none of his male friends. He despised ignorant people, and didn't like trifling and small-talk. He didn't like dark-skinned people. . . . He was not well balanced: he had too much brain. He scoffed at everything sacred, and never went to church. . . . He said often that there was a mystery hanging over him he never could fathom. He believed he was born to suffer, and this embittered his whole life. Mrs. Clemm also spoke vaguely of some family mystery, of some disgrace.[43]

While none of Starr's assertions is shocking, Poe does come across as unusually irascible and judgmental in her portrait. Does "dark-skinned people" refer to African Americans? "Negroes" would have been a much more common term (in both the 1830s and 1889, when the interview was published); and why would she even mention that Poe didn't like black people, given the pervasive racism of the time? It suggests to me that Poe's prejudice extended to other "dark-skinned" ethnic groups or to immigrants generally. The sense of mystery and the belief that he was "born to suffer" are certainly echoed in Poe's early poetry, and, given the tragedy and disappointments he had already experienced, that outlook is not too surprising.

Starr's account also supports the assumption that Poe did not hold down a steady job, at least not in the year or so that they were seeing each other.[44] "Eddie was never educated to work," she remembered. "He was very proud and sensitive." He was also sober for the most part, a claim made not only by Starr but also by another friend from Baltimore, Lambert Wilmer.[45] However, drinking did contribute to Poe's breakup with Starr: he showed up at her house much later than expected one night, intoxicated. They argued; then Mary got scared and tried to get away from him. According to Starr, when her mother intervened, Poe claimed he had a right to see her because "she is my wife now in the sight of Heaven." In attributing this statement to Poe, her insinuation seemed to be that they had had sexual relations; she also said that "he would just as lief have lived with a woman without being married to her." Though much of her reminiscence of Poe is sympathetic, she believed she had made "a narrow escape" by not marrying him.

Starr mentioned that in the aftermath of their breakup, Poe had his young cousin Virginia deliver messages to her. In fact, Poe was becoming increasingly attached to Virginia, and to his Aunt Maria. Starr described Virginia, who was probably ten or eleven years old at the time, as "delicate. . . . Her sole beauty was in the expression of her face. Her disposition was lovely. She had violet eyes, dark brown hair, and a bad complexion that spoiled her looks." People who knew Virginia later in life do not say that her looks were in any way spoiled, but otherwise suggest that she remained much as Starr described her: graceful and childlike, with dark hair and dark eyes. She added that an Virginia already was very fond of Poe, "as any child would be of anybody that paid her attention."[46] The fondness was mutual: regarding her as more sister than cousin, Poe began calling Virginia "Sissy." Poe's friend Lambert Wilmer later recalled walking with him and Virginia "in the neighborhood of Baltimore" when they encountered a funeral. While listening to the obsequies, "Virginia became affected and shed more tears than the chief mourner. Her emotion communicated itself to Poe" and he too became greatly moved at the service for a stranger.[47] Especially after the death of Henry, Poe must have been more inclined to cling to his young cousin, who in turn looked up to him.

At some point in 1833, the family moved from Mechanics Row to No. 3 North Amity Street in West Baltimore (now numbered 203 N. Amity, one of the three Poe houses that have been preserved). The reason for the move is uncertain, but it seems likely that cheaper rent was a motivation, given the family's strained finances. The Clemm-Poe family's new residence, half of a recently built duplex, was on the edge of town, about a mile and a half west of central Baltimore. Although they had the entire house, two floors and an attic, the structure was very small—about six hundred square feet—possibly no larger than the upper-floor living space of their previous home. The family endured a Spartan existence on the urban frontier: streetlights did not extend that far from the city center, and water would have to be carried from a nearby well or canal.[48] The first-floor fireplace was surely inadequate for providing heat to upstairs bedrooms.

Living in poverty, Poe was determined to advance his career. Lambert Wilmer later recalled that his friend was "constantly occupied with his literary labors" during this period, but, again, he was bringing in almost no income.[49] In the spring of 1835, he asked his friend Kennedy to recommend him for a teaching position at a public school, telling him that "in my present circumstances such a situation would be most desirable."[50] Poe did not get the teaching job, but Kennedy proved helpful in making another connection:

Figure 2.4 The house where Poe and his family lived in Baltimore for more than two years, 1833–35 (left); Poe's bedroom as it is displayed today.

with Thomas Willis White, the editor of a new Richmond magazine called the *Southern Literary Messenger*. Kennedy told White about Poe's still unpublished "volume of very bizarre tales" and informed him that he had "turned [Poe] to drudging upon whatever may make money."[51] Poe began corresponding with White, promoting the *Messenger* with blurbs in other publications and contributing new stories.

In March, White published Poe's "Berenice," a macabre tale that continued to display his fascination with death proving to be other than what it seems. The story's narrator develops an obsession with his dying wife's teeth. The night following her burial, in a kind of somnambulist trance, he disinters her, and, upon waking, discovers not only that he has extracted her teeth but also that he did the hideous deed while she still lived, for she had been mistakenly buried alive. White worried about publishing such a cringe-inducing story, but Poe, even as he apologized for it, insisted that weird, sensational fiction would attract readers to the magazine. He described this popular mode as "the ludicrous heightened into the grotesque: the fearful coloured into the horrible: the witty exaggerated into the burlesque: the singular wrought out into the strange and mystical" (L 1:84). Indeed, along with plots that straddle the line between life and death, these extreme stylistic mash-ups characterize almost all of Poe's early fiction. In "Morella," his next story for the *Messenger*, the title character is an unloved wife who dies in childbirth; as her daughter reaches puberty, the father recognizes her as a kind of replica of her mother. He loves his daughter dearly, but, when he acknowledges the uncanny resemblance, speaking the name "Morella," it is as if he has resurrected his wife. "I am here!" answers the daughter, just before she dies. "With my own hands," the father tells us, "I bore her to the tomb; and I laughed with a long and bitter laugh as I found no traces of the first, in the charnel where I laid the second—Morella" (T 1:236).

Back in the real world, Poe's grandmother Elizabeth Carines Poe died on July 8, 1835, and the annuity she had been receiving for her husband's Revolutionary War service went with her, creating a true financial crisis for the household. Maria's son Henry (not to be confused with Poe's brother) had set out on his own, either in Baltimore or at sea, leaving just Edgar, Maria, and Virginia. Poe could hardly continue to draw on the family's meager resources now, but, fortunately, he had recently received an offer from Thomas White to help edit the *Messenger* in Richmond. He moved there in late July or early August, but he did not want to live apart from Maria and Virginia. Having lost his parents in early childhood and, more recently, his foster parents, Poe was desperate to keep the familial love and support that had grown throughout the four years he had lived with the Clemms. Maria, whom Poe called "Muddy," now regarded him as a son, and his affection for Virginia had developed into a romantic attachment. He broached the possibility of marriage, despite her being only thirteen, half his age.

Poe wanted his aunt and cousin to move to Richmond, but he now faced a new obstacle. Neilson Poe, Edgar's prosperous second cousin and a Baltimore resident, volunteered to take in Virginia, support her and educate her. When Maria informed Poe of Neilson's generous offer, he replied from Richmond with a frantic, pleading letter:

> I have procured a sweet little house in a retired situation on [ch]urch hill . . . I have been dreaming every day & night since of the rapture I should feel in [hav]ing my only friends—all I love on Earth with me there, [and] the pride I would take in making you both comfort[able] & in calling her my wife—But the dream is over[.] [Oh G]od have mercy on me. What have I *to live for*? Among strangers with *not one soul to love me.* (L 1:102–3)

He added a postscript to Virginia: "My love, my own sweetest Sissy, my darling little wifey, thi[nk w]ell before you break the heart of your cousin. Eddy" (L 1:104). There is no getting around the strangeness of Poe's determination to marry his young cousin. While marriage between first cousins was not taboo in 1830s America, marriage between a twenty-six-year-old man and a thirteen-year-old girl was certainly unusual.[52] Neilson might have made his offer specifically to block Poe's marriage plans, assuming he knew of them, but it is also possible that Poe proposed the marriage to counter the possibility of Virginia joining Neilson's family. Either way, was Poe clinging to a sister ("Sissy") and mother ("Muddy") or to a prospective wife and *her* mother? These relationships were not clearly delineated for Poe, as suggested by his use of the cloying phrase "my darling little wifey."[53]

As his stunningly dramatic letter to Maria suggests, Poe was deeply shaken by the possibility of living without her and Virginia. Two weeks later, he wrote to Kennedy, thanking him for his help in getting the *Messenger* job but also confiding that he was seriously depressed, even hinting at suicide. He didn't point to the possible family rupture as the cause, but he sounded as desperate as he did in his letter to Maria: "Write me immediately. Convince me that it is worth one's while—that it is at all necessary to live, and you will prove yourself indeed my friend" (L 1:107). Soon after, Poe left White and Richmond, heading back to Baltimore, where he and Virginia may have been married privately: a license was issued on September 22. Poe then prevailed upon White to reinstate him and moved, with Virginia and Maria, back to Richmond in early October. Although he would never live in Baltimore again, he would visit many times, and would even claim the city, at least implicitly, as another hometown: providing biographical information for a publication years later, he wrote, "Born January, 1811. Family one of the oldest and most respectable in Baltimore." Poe seems to have encouraged the belief that he was not only two years younger than he was, but also a Baltimorean.[54]

Edgar, Virginia, and Maria would spend the next fifteen months in Richmond. They moved into a boarding house run by a Mrs. Martha Yarrington on Bank Street, facing the state capitol. At nine dollars a week, this was relatively expensive lodging. They hoped Maria could establish a boardinghouse of her own: Poe secured funds from two distant cousins, William Poe in Alabama and George Poe Jr., in Georgia, for that purpose. At one point he made an agreement with his boss, Thomas White, to rent a house from him and board both his and White's family, but the house proved too small. There is no record of the family having lived anywhere else in Richmond. On May 16, 1836, Edgar and Virginia, who was now fourteen, were married publicly at the Yarrington house. Having blocked Neilson Poe's plan to shelter Virginia back in Baltimore, Poe had effectively become the head of the household. In a letter to William Poe soon after their arrival in Richmond, Maria described herself and Virginia as "entirely dependent on Edgar," who was "indeed a son to me."[55] To George Poe a few months later (but still before the marriage ceremony), she described them as "under the protection of Edgar."[56]

Living literally in the center of town, Poe surely saw and felt traces of his former life in Richmond, with all its losses and disappointments, wherever he turned. Mrs. Yarrington's house was just a few blocks from the house where, as a child, Poe had lived with the Allans before their English sojourn, and about half a mile east of Moldavia, the urban mansion where John Allan's widow and her family still resided. Shockoe Hill Cemetery, the burial place not only of Helen Stanard and Frances Allan but now also of John Allan, was about a mile and a half to the north, while St. John's Churchyard, where his mother was interred in an unmarked grave, was about a mile to the east. He could walk to the *Messenger* office at Fifteenth and Main in less than five minutes.

From that small office, Poe launched the next phase of his career as an editor and critic, with a series of reviews and articles that drew national attention. His justification of the gory "Berenice" applied equally to his take-no-prisoners approach to book reviewing. Combining sarcasm, overstatement, and close reading, he made literary reviews entertaining and comic, while raising the hackles of old-fashioned editors. "Well!—here we have it! This is *the* book—*the* book *par excellence*—the book bepuffed, beplastered, and be-*Mirrored*": so begins Poe's take-down of the novel *Norman Leslie* by Theodore S. Fay, an editor of the *New York Mirror* and thus a well-connected figure in Gotham's literary establishment. Poe goes on to mock the hype and the pretense of anonymity surrounding Fay's novel, referring specifically to what was known as "puffing," or indiscrimi-

Figure 2.5 An archival photograph of the building at Fifteenth and East Main Streets, Richmond, Virginia, that housed the *Southern Literary Messenger*, Poe's workplace from 1835 to early 1837, blended with a contemporary photograph of the corner. (Archival photograph courtesy of the Valentine, Richmond, Virginia.)

nately praising the work of writers within one's circle: "For the sake of everything puffed, puffing, and puffable, let us take a peep at its contents!" (ER 540). Poe takes more than a peep, ridiculing the novel mercilessly as he summarizes its plot, pronouncing it "the most inestimable piece of balderdash with which the common sense of the good people of America was ever so openly or so villainously insulted!" (ER 546). The young editor had nothing to lose, attacking a powerful New York literary clique from the distant cultural outpost of Richmond. His attacks won him the attention he craved: magazines and weekly papers regularly exchanged copies to ensure that editors knew what their competitors were up to, and they commented regularly in print, essentially reviewing each other. Though opinions were divided over

Poe's tactics, he embraced the image of the "Tomahawk Man," as he would soon be known.

Poe wrote little new fiction while editing the *Messenger*, but he republished most of the stories he had written in Baltimore, giving them a second, wider audience. And, along with his reviews, he embraced other attention-grabbing forms of nonfiction writing. In April 1836, he published a detailed exposé of a chess-playing automaton, a "machine" constructed to look like a man, with human reasoning skills. Although Poe's conclusion—that a lever-pulling assistant was hidden inside the contraption—was no great revelation, his point-by-point analysis of the presentation and the architecture of deception reinforced his image as a rigorous critic while prefiguring the "raciocinative" method of his later detective fiction. In another feature, he decoded the signatures of well-known writers, posing as an autograph collector who deduces authors' personal characteristics and abilities from the way they sign their names. Thus, the combative outsider-insider pose that he adopted with "The Folio Club" was on display throughout his writing for *Messenger*.

But, by the close of 1836, Poe and Thomas White were already near the end of their productive collaboration. Although Poe would later claim to have increased the *Messenger*'s subscription list almost eightfold during his editorship, the magazine's growth, while healthy, was a more modest 40 percent, from about 1300 to 1800 subscribers.[57] That margin might not have been enough to calm White's concerns about Poe's irascible editorial persona; White, who was more publisher than editor, and much less of a writer, also tussled with Poe over questions of editorial control. But it was probably Poe's personal behavior that bothered White the most. In some ways, their relationship mirrored that of John Allan and his foster son: impressed as he was with Poe's abilities, White recognized what he regarded as character flaws—most significant, occasional drunkenness—not long after Poe joined him in the office. Poe left him in the lurch when he returned temporarily to Baltimore in late 1835, and White made his staying sober a condition of reinstatement, suggesting that Richmond itself was a bad influence: "Edgar, when you once again tread these streets, I have my fears that your resolve will fall through,—and that you would again sip the juice, even till it stole away your senses."[58] By this point in his life, at age twenty-six Edgar was well aware that he had a low tolerance for alcohol and was unable to drink moderately, safe only when he abstained altogether. But as White pointed out, the "social" drinking endemic to Richmond (and any other US city) was a constant temptation.

A year later their relationship was again at the breaking point, and White wrote to another associate, the novelist and jurist Nathaniel Beverly Tucker, "Poe pesters me no little—he is trying every manoeuvre to foist himself on some one at the North. . . . He is continually after me for money. I am as sick of his writings, as I am of him,—and am rather more than half inclined to send him up another dozen dollars in the morning, and along with it all his unpublished manuscripts."[59] For his part, Poe referred to White in an 1840 letter as "illiterate and vulgar, although well-meaning" (L 1:236). Much as he had done ten years earlier in his break with Allan, Poe set out from Richmond for an unknown future. In both 1827 and 1837, he effectively disappeared—the first time into the army, where he became Edgar Perry, this next time into poverty and obscurity in New York City.

Whether Poe was fired by White or quit, he was willing to give up a steady-paying editorial position and try his luck in New York. Perhaps Richmond harbored too many ghosts for him. Poe had certainly come to feel underpaid and underappreciated by White, but he also must have sensed that bigger things were happening in his chosen profession up north, where, as White said, he would try to "foist himself" upon some other magazine proprietor. Unfortunately for biographers, 1837 and early 1838 offer few clues as to his whereabouts or activities. What is known is that he, Virginia, and Maria left Richmond for New York in February, and that they lived first in a house at Sixth Avenue and Waverly Place, near Washington Square, and then moved a few blocks further down Sixth Avenue to 113 ½ Carmine Street. One of these dwellings might have been a boarding-house run by Maria; a bookseller named William Gowans later recalled living with the family for eight months, and reported that Poe was "one of the most courteous, gentlemanly, and intelligent companions I have met with during my journeyings and haltings through divers divisions of the globe."[60]

But early 1837 turned out to be a particularly bad time to move to New York: a financial panic ushered in an almost decade-long recession, of which Gotham was the epicenter. New York banks suspended specie payments for paper currency in May. The real-estate bubble burst, businesses folded, and the city's dizzying growth temporarily ground to a halt.[61] Before leaving the *Messenger*, Poe had begun what was supposed to be a serialized sea adventure, *The Narrative of Arthur Gordon Pym*, but he gave White only two installments. Harper & Brothers agreed to publish the complete novel not long after Poe arrived in New York, announcing it as "nearly ready for publication" in April. But the novel did not appear for another fifteen months, as the Harpers curtailed their publications in the wake of the panic. Poe might have been writing steadily, but he published almost nothing in the year after leaving Richmond. Prior to the financial panic, still hopeful that his reputation as a fearless critic would lead to greater fame as a "magazinist," he attended a New York publishers' dinner for booksellers and proposed a toast "to the *Monthlies* of Gotham." Almost nothing else is known of Poe's first New York residence (he would return in 1844; see chapter 4), but that very lack of evidence suggests that it was a difficult year. Having transformed himself into a fiction writer in Baltimore and a caustic reviewer in Richmond, he had developed the skills to succeed in the literary marketplace. But, throughout 1837, all he could do was survive, along with his teenage bride and her doting mother, until it was time to start a new chapter in a new town.

CHAPTER 3

Philadelphia (1838–1844)

By early 1838, Poe's once-promising career as a writer, critic, and editor had stalled in New York City, largely because of the Panic of 1837, which stymied the publishing sector along with the rest of the economy. Although the panic's effects would radiate from New York throughout the northeast, it was still probably wise to try another city. Poe and family relocated to Philadelphia, hoping to meet with better fortune in what was then the second city of publishing and, arguably, the first for magazine publishing. And, to a great extent, he succeeded: professionally and artistically, Poe hit his stride during the next six years, eventually editing one of the nation's highest-circulation magazines while writing most of the tales on which his modern reputation rests. He also became part of a professional and social network that surrounded his trade. By his own standards, his domestic life was stable as well, at least for a while: along with Virginia and Maria ("Sissy" and "Muddy"), he apparently managed to stay in the same house for almost four of their six years there. The trio's devotion to each other deepened: Poe loved his wife dearly, and he came to think of Maria as his own mother. And yet success as a writer and editor did not lift Poe's family out of poverty; he continued to be thwarted by his alcoholism and professional combativeness, and personal misfortune continued to haunt him throughout his Philadelphia years.

Like New York, Philadelphia saw its rapid economic development temporarily derailed by the Panic of 1837, and the city would continue to experience deflated wages and prices until the mid-1840s. In 1842, one well-off Philadelphian, Sidney George Fisher, would opine, "The streets seem deserted, the largest houses are shut up and to rent, there is no business, there is no money, no confidence & little hope . . . nobody can pay debts, the miseries of poverty are felt both by rich & poor, [and] everyone you see looks careworn and haggard."[1] This would have been a familiar scene for Poe, who had not found steady employment in New York. Meanwhile, Harper & Brothers had to delay the publication of his novel *The Narrative of Arthur Gordon Pym* for about a year, so the book he began in Richmond and completed in New York would not appear until his first year in Philadelphia.

But Fisher's description of a penniless, hopeless town tells only part of Philadelphia's story in the late 1830s and early 1840s. The city's population was still growing, most rapidly in the new districts to the south, west, and north than in the city center. The metropolitan area (which would become incorporated in 1854) grew dramatically, from 161,410 residents in 1830 to 565,529 in 1860. The population of suburban Spring Garden—the area north of Vine St. where Poe would move in 1843—more than doubled, from just under 28,000 to almost 59,000, in the 1840s alone.[2] Philadelphia had become an industrial city in the 1830s, embracing coal, steam, canals, and railways; the panic would not stop the revolution that concentrated textile mills and heavy industry near the Delaware River.[3] In addition to new factories and mills, Philadelphians took pride in the state-of-the-art waterworks completed in the 1820s on the Schuylkill River, northwest of the city.[4] A short walk from the waterworks, Eastern State Penitentiary, designed by John Haviland, opened in 1829 and became a controversial model for the modern prison. Haviland and other architects such as

William Strickland and Thomas U. Walter had transformed the cityscape in the years before the panic with grand structures of marble and granite, including the Second Bank of the United States, the US Mint, and the Philadelphia Arcade, as well as numerous churches and private homes.[5]

Largely because of these stately structures and the city's well-established grid streetscape, visitors frequently remarked on the orderliness and "regularity" of Philadelphia and the continuing influence of its Quaker heritage. Charles Dickens invoked both of these tropes—somewhat negatively—in his description of the city in 1842: "It is a handsome city, but distractingly regular. After walking about it for an hour or two, I felt that I would have given the world for a crooked street. The collar of my coat appeared to stiffen, and the brim of my hat to expand, beneath its quakerly influence. My hair shrunk into a sleek short crop, my hands folded themselves upon my breast of their own calm accord."[6] But profound instability not only lurked beneath that superficial decorum and regularity; it surfaced frequently. Historian Elizabeth Geffen attributes the "unprecedented civic violence" of the period to the rapid increase in population, which threw together disparate racial and ethnic groups, as well as widening inequality and a lack of decent housing.[7] The city saw frequent strikes and other collective protests—for instance, vandalizing railroads to thwart the routing of new lines through a residential area—as well as violence associated with volunteer firemen's clubs and street gangs.[8] Still more disturbing was the sustained terrorist violence rooted in xenophobia and racism, which fueled at least five riots between 1834 and 1844. In May 1838, around the time Poe and family arrived, a mob burned down the newly built Pennsylvania Hall, a center of reform activity that had recently hosted a lecture by abolitionist Angelina Grimké. Firemen protected adjacent buildings but allowed the hall to collapse as a crowd gathered to watch. The following night, an African American orphanage was destroyed by a mob.[9] The year Poe left for New York, 1844, at least fifteen people would be killed and dozens injured in nativist riots throughout Philadelphia.

Less visible than the dignified public structures, new construction often meant building in back lots while subdividing old houses into tenements, so that the orderly façade of the city's broader streets hid slapdash architecture and often squalid living conditions.[10] An 1849 Sanitary Commission report describes "badly contrived houses, crowded by occupants, filthy and poor, without ventilation or drainage, or receptacles for refuse, or supply of water, or the common comforts of life."[11] This dynamic of an orderly, "regular" city hiding disorder, struggling to contain its own violent propensities, was at the heart of the most popular American novel of the first half of the century: *The Quaker City; or the Monks of Monk Hall,* by Poe's friend and fellow Philadelphian George Lippard. A complex, lurid potboiler, Lippard's 1844 novel sensationalizes and gothicizes the social conditions of Philadelphia during Poe's time there. Monk Hall, where much of the novel's action takes place, symbolizes Philadelphia's corruption and depravity; frequented by superficially respectable gentlemen, it serves as the hub of the city's network of dark schemes and sexual violence.[12]

Poe's life during these years was deeply enmeshed in the flux and contradictions of mid-century Philadelphia. With Sissy and Muddy, he settled into a boarding house at 202 Mulberry (now Arch) Street run by a Mrs. Jones upon his arrival in early 1838. In or around September, they moved to what Poe described only as a "small house," which he later called the "old place," located probably in the vicinity of Sixteenth Street and Locust.[13] The move itself typified a local demographic trend in that Poe left the old part of town,

Figure 3.1 This 1857 lithograph depicting a "Bird's-Eye View of Philadelphia" postdates Poe's time there by a little more than a decade, but conveys a sense of the city's movement from the shore of the Delaware River (background) toward the Schuylkill River (foreground) and the northern suburbs (to the left). (Courtesy of the Library of Congress, Prints and Photographs Division, LC-DIG-pga-03107.)

near the Delaware River, which was increasingly commercial and industrial, for the western half of the grid, closer to the Schuylkill. Philadelphia's population was moving in that direction, shifting the city's center: the portion of its inhabitants living west of Seventh Street increased from about 40 percent in 1830 to 60 percent in 1840.[14] Poe and his family had moved to an area that for another decade or so might be considered the outskirts, about two blocks east of Rittenhouse Square. As contemporary maps show, the blocks around the square were not yet built up in the early 1840s. Affluent citizens had begun building homes west of

Broad Street, but Poe's part of town remained semirural and working class. When the wealthy lawyer Philip Physick commissioned John Haviland to design a house at Nineteenth and Walnut, the resulting Greek Revival mansion was dubbed "Physick's Folly" for its incongruity with the undeveloped, hardscrabble surroundings.[15] Poe, Virginia, and Maria lived four or five blocks away and probably watched the grand house being built across the barren Rittenhouse Square. This sparsely populated section of the Eighth Ward was transitioning, however. In the 1830s, gas street lamps and cobblestone pavements had been installed on the more heavily traveled streets from the Delaware to the Schuylkill, and horse-drawn omnibuses ran the length of the east-west thoroughfare of High (now Market) Street starting in 1836.[16]

Unfortunately, almost no reliable information survives concerning Poe's own habitation on Philadelphia's urban frontier. In fact, a reminiscence of Anne E. C. Clarke, the daughter of publisher and Poe associate Thomas Clarke, is the sole source for locating the family at Sixteenth and Locust. In letters from this period, Poe reports that he is still at "the old place," then later refers to having moved in 1842 from "the old place." An 1875 magazine article by Amanda B. Harris, who knew a woman who had known the family, describes a "little rose-covered cottage on the outskirts of Philadelphia," but it isn't clear whether she is referring to the "old place" or to one of Poe's later residences. The more significant detail Harris provides is that the family was reluctantly accepting charity from a group of women (which included her acquaintance) who had organized relief efforts for neighbors in need.[17]

Poe had been in difficult, often desperate financial straits since leaving West Point in 1831, his time as editor of the

BURTON'S

GENTLEMAN'S MAGAZINE.

EDITED BY

WILLIAM E. BURTON AND EDGAR A. POE.

VOLUME V.

FROM JULY TO DECEMBER.

By a gentleman, we mean not to draw a line that would be invidious between high and low, rank and subordination, riches and poverty. No. *The distinction is in the mind.* Whoever is open, just, and true; whoever is of a humane and affable demeanor; whoever is honorable in himself, and in his judgment of others, and requires no law but his word to make him fulfil an engagement;—such a man is a gentleman;—and such a man may be found among the tillers of the earth as well as in the drawing rooms of the high born and the rich.
De Vere.

PHILADELPHIA.
PUBLISHED BY WILLIAM E. BURTON,
DOCK STREET, OPPOSITE THE EXCHANGE

1839.

Figure 3.2 Title page for a six-month volume of *Burton's Gentleman's Magazine*, which included Poe's stories "William Wilson," "The Man That Was Used Up," and "The Fall of the House of Usher."

Southern Literary Messenger having provided the only brief respite. His frustration over the family's poverty is underscored by a request he made in July 1838 to James Kirke Paulding, an author and newly appointed secretary of the navy with whom Poe had corresponded while working at the *Messenger*:

> Could I obtain the most unimportant Clerkship in your gift—*any thing, by sea or land*—to relieve me from the miserable life of literary drudgery to which I now, with a break-

ing heart, submit, and for which neither my temper nor my abilities have fitted me, I would never again repine at any dispensation of God. I feel that I could then, (having something beyond mere literature as a profession) quickly elevate myself to the station in society which is my due. It is needless to say how fervent, how unbounded would be my gratitude to the one who should thus rescue me from ruin, and put me in possession of happiness. (L 1:175)

While Poe would complain throughout his career about the mistreatment of authors in the publishing marketplace, the Paulding letter is rare in its suggestion that he would actually abandon "literature as a profession" if he could. At this point, Poe just wanted a "white collar" job that would provide for his household. Not that a clerkship would preclude literary writing altogether, but his anguish at this point seems to have been as dire as it had been in Baltimore. Paulding did not come to Poe's rescue.

Though he might have been willing to give up the literary life for a decently remunerative clerkship, Poe had moved to Philadelphia to advance his career as a writer and editor, and he had come to the right place. By 1838 Philadelphia supported over a dozen daily and weekly newspapers, including the *Pennsylvania* (later *Philadelphia*) *Inquirer*, the *North American*, and the city's first penny paper, the *Public Ledger*.[18] Prominent weeklies included the *Saturday Museum*, *Alexander's Weekly Messenger*, the *Dollar Newspaper*, and the *Saturday Courier*, all of which published Poe's work in the late 1830s and early 1840s. While manuscripts could be sent by mail, Poe would have wanted to establish a physical presence among local publishers. He had moved to the west side of town for cheaper rent, but Philadelphia was still enough of a walking city that he could easily reach the offices of the city's book, newspaper, and magazine publishers in less than half an hour—including *Godey's Lady's*

Book, the most successful national monthly magazine of the period, and Lea & Blanchard, the firm that reluctantly issued Poe's *Tales of the Grotesque and Arabesque* in 1840.[19]

In May 1839, over two years after leaving the *Messenger*, Poe finally found steady work with a recently launched Philadelphia monthly, *Burton's Gentleman's Magazine*. William E. Burton, its founder, was a popular actor for whom editing and publishing proved to be a temporary sideline. As had been the case at the *Messenger* with Thomas White, at *Burton's* Poe was employed to assist someone with less understanding of magazines and literature than himself. Not surprisingly, similar frictions came into play, and the arrangement lasted only about a year. Still, the job was what Poe needed at the time, even if it paid less than a government clerkship. *Burton's* provided Poe with an outlet for his acerbic literary criticism and innovative new stories, notably "The Fall of the House of Usher," "The Man That Was Used Up," and "The Man of the Crowd" (all published in 1839–40). He also reprinted many of his previously published tales and poems, bringing them to a new audience. While the image of Benjamin Franklin on the magazine's title page attested to its Philadelphian origin, *Burton's* was not at all provincial in its content, which included essays on history, travel, and pastimes as well as fiction, poetry, and criticism. Like other monthlies, it included full-page engraved illustrations (or "plates"), was printed on good quality paper, and would typically be bound handsomely in six-month volumes to be preserved by its subscribers.

The job of Assistant Editor at *Burton's* gave Poe an entrée into the publishing, legal, and political worlds of Philadelphia. In fact, these "worlds" were essentially one old-fashioned boys' club, as the periodical press and partisan politics were inextricable. Poe's friend Jesse E. Dow, a frequent contributor to *Burton's*, was a prominent Locofoco (i.e.,

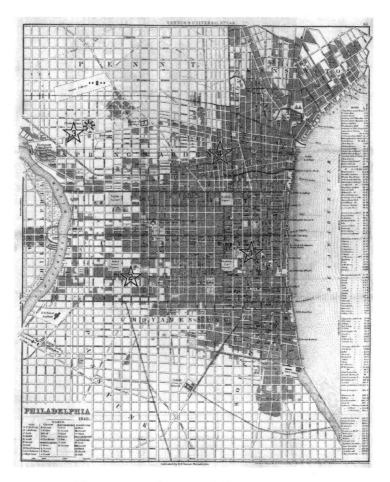

Figure 3.3 This 1840 map by Henry S. Tanner Jr., represents Philadelphia two years after Poe moved there. The locations of Poe's first boardinghouse (1), the "old place" near Rittenhouse Square (2), the house in Fairmount (3), and the house in Spring Garden (4) are marked. (Courtesy of David Rumsey Historical Map Collection, www.davidrumsey.com.)

radical) Democrat. A poet, editor, and journalist, Dow (like Nathaniel Hawthorne eight years later) lost his Custom House appointment in 1841 after the election of a new president—in this case, William Henry Harrison, of the more conservative, pro-business-and-banking Whig Party. George Lippard was a socialist journalist-editor as well as a novelist; he wrote regularly for the Democratic newspaper *Spirit of the Times*, then edited his own short-lived *Citizen Soldier*. Poe was also friendly with *Spirit of the Times*'s editor, John Stephenson DuSolle.

On the Whig side, where Poe's political sympathies generally resided, there was Frederick W. Thomas, a Cincinnati novelist and editor who befriended Poe on a visit to Philadelphia and became a frequent correspondent. Thomas Dunn English, a friend who would later become a bitter enemy, was a lawyer and writer prominent in local Whig politics. Henry Beck Hirst—horticultural merchant, lawyer, poet, and a close friend of T. D. English—was described by engraver and publisher John Sartain as Poe's "rollicking companion"; Lippard would satirize English and Hirst in the *Spirit of the Times*, renaming them Thomas Dunn Brown and Henry Bread Crust.[20] On at least one occasion, Poe rubbed elbows with the most eminent Philadelphian of his day: Nicholas Biddle, who had been a magazine editor himself early in his career, served as president of the Second Bank of the United States, squaring off against president Andrew Jackson in the "Bank War" that led up to the Panic of 1837. In 1841, when Poe wrote to Biddle asking him to write an article for his prospective magazine, he referred to "the kind manner in which you received me when I called upon you at [Biddle's suburban estate] Andalusia" (CL 1:254).

Magazine work was essential to the social and political culture of Philadelphia and the nation; moreover, it was a vital sector of the economy. The explosion of magazines and cheap newspapers was driven by an urban population that was increasing at a rate three times that of the population as a whole.[21] The market for periodicals, which provided everything from news and commercial information to history lessons and musical scores, could barely keep up with the demands of city dwellers. Newspapers and magazines provided not only a way to fill short periods of time throughout the day but also the possibility of community in an urban "world of strangers."[22] At the same time, printing newspapers and magazines in greater quantities became easier and less expensive thanks to improvements in technology, including steam-driven presses and machine-made paper. In the second quarter of the nineteenth century, which includes Poe's entire career, 2,871 magazines were founded in the United States; most were short-lived, but even so, the number of magazines in print rose from 212 in 1825 to 776 in 1850.[23]

We tend to associate the word "magazine" with general-interest, middle-brow publications (the best example in Poe's time being *Godey's*), but their proliferation was driven by a wide range of specialized interests, suggesting a parallel with the cultural impact of the internet at the dawn of the twenty-first century. As early as 1831, one editor described the medium's pervasiveness:

> Nothing can be done without them. Sects and parties, benevolent societies, and ingenious individuals, all have their periodicals. . . . Every man, and every party, that seeks to establish a new theory, or to break down an old one, commences operations, like a board of war, by founding a *magazine*. We have annuals, monthlys, and weeklys—reviews, orthodox and heterodox—journals of education and humanity, of law, divinity and physic—magazines for ladies and for gentlemen—publications commercial, mechanical, metaphysical, sentimental, musical, anti-dogmatical, and nonsensical.[24]

These claims sound familiar: a revolution in information technology democratizes publishing while creating seemingly countless niche audiences. And yet, one significant respect in which the "first golden age of magazines" (as the period has frequently been called) does *not* resemble the internet age is that the means of production and dissemination in the 1830s and 1840s were still concentrated in just a few large northeastern cities—namely, New York, Boston, and Philadelphia.[25]

Having cut his teeth writing for periodicals while living in Baltimore and Richmond, Poe now thrived—artistically, if not financially—as a writer of riveting tales, made for magazines. "Ligeia," "William Wilson," and "The Fall of the House of Usher," all published within the first eighteen months of his arrival in Philadelphia, are ingeniously constructed gothic stories that defy simple interpretation. Each one deploys a supernatural motif (a dead woman's revivification; a doppelgänger; a living, sentient house) to explore the workings of obsession, conscience, guilt, and self-loathing. While in Philadelphia, Poe articulated a theory of the short story based on "unity of effect": the brevity of a tale would become, for Poe, its great asset, its mechanism for the author's control over the reader. He would demonstrate this theory through stories such as "Ligeia," "William Wilson," and "Usher," as well as "The Masque of the Red Death," "The Pit and the Pendulum," "The Black Cat," and "The Tell-Tale Heart." All were written in Philadelphia in the early 1840s, and all were sold to magazines, the medium that for Poe had come to define a new kind of literature: "The curt, the terse, the well-timed, and the readily diffused, in preference to the old forms of the verbose and ponderous & the inaccessible" (L 1:467).

Along with stories steeped in gothicism or otherwise eliciting terror, Poe continued to devise other "effects" through fiction, particularly satire. Several of Poe's stories from his first years in Philadelphia reflect the contradictions and anxieties gnawing at the culture of order and success that periodical publishing reflected and participated in. Published in *Burton's* in November 1838, "The Psyche Zenobia" (later retitled "How to Write a Blackwood Article" and "A Predicament") lampoons women writers as well as the "sensation tales" associated with *Blackwood's Edinburgh Magazine*, but it also contains this description of how the magazine's "political articles" are "managed": "Mr. Blackwood has a pair of tailor's-shears, and three apprentices who stand by him for orders. One hands him the 'Times,' another the 'Examiner,' and third a 'Gulley's New Compendium of Slang-Whang.' Mr. B. merely cuts out and intersperses. It is soon done—nothing but Examiner, Slam-Whang, and Times—then Times, Slam-Whang, and Examiner—and then Times, Examiner, and Slam-Whang" (T 1:338). Poe implies that political articles are composed through a combination of plagiarism and chance; no actual writing takes place. Instead, Mr. Blackwood "manages" content, imitating a machine in the production of text that is either a collage of recycled opinion or, more likely, total nonsense. Public discourse in the mass media age of the mid-nineteenth century is presented here as a humbug: there is no need to write when readers won't know the difference between individual expression and a cut-and-paste, assembly-line product—they look alike on the printed page.

Poe's 1840 satire "Peter Pendulum, the Business Man" is more overtly tied to Philadelphia; written in imitation of the Philadelphia writer John Neal's *Charcoal Sketches*, its narrator also caricatures that shrewd entrepreneur Benjamin Franklin. Peter Pendulum (significantly, renamed Peter Proffit in later versions) insists that he is "a methodical man," and repeatedly uses the words "method" and "system" as the touchstones of his business success; he disdains "genius," which he regards as their opposite. The joke is that Pendulum's "method" is always petty and dishonest. He first freelances as a walking advertisement for a tailor's shop, attracting customers by modeling clothes in public but also lying about the quality of the material. The bill he presents to "Mssrs. Cut and Comeagain, Merchant Tailors," itemizes the lies he tells to customers; he also charges more for bringing fat customers to the store than medium or small ones. His subsequent ventures are even more blatant perversions of free enterprise, as they amount to being paid to remove nuisances of his own creation. He builds "eye-sore" hovels next to sites of grand new construction so that the owners will pay him to take down the offending structures. He goads men into assaulting him so that he can sue them or settle out of court. Finally, he takes up "mud-dabbling," stationing himself on a muddy street corner with a broom in order to collect protection money from passersby who prefer not to be splattered. Under cover of smug businessman's cant about adhering to a method, Poe's Mr. Pendulum equates getting ahead in business with swindling or extortion, the inverse of creating value or contributing to society. His last sentences liken Pendulum's petty maneuvers to the institutions that were actually reshaping the American economy. He boasts that his "method" exempted no one from mud-dabbling: "Never imposing upon any one myself, I suffered no one to play the possum with me. The frauds of the banks of course I couldn't help. Their suspension put me to ruinous inconvenience. These, however, are not individuals, but corporations; and corporations, it is very well known, have neither bodies to be kicked, nor souls to be damned" (T 1:488–89).

In other words, the economic effects of bank failures trickled down even to *his* profession, but in broader terms,

Mr. Pendulum recognizes that as frauds go, he is no match for banks and corporations, against whose bodiless, soulless entities no retribution can be taken.

A more complex satire, "The Man That Was Used Up"—also first published in *Burton's*—focuses on a different sort of bodiless, soulless entity, but it, too, exposes the paltry con game behind a grandiose façade. The universally admired Indian fighter Brevet Brigadier General John A.B.C. Smith displays physical perfection, described by a fawning narrator fascinated by the General's "fine shoulders," the "handsomest pair of whiskers under the sun," "the *ne plus ultra* of good legs," and so on (T 1:379). General Smith tirelessly celebrates "the rapid march of mechanical invention" and the superiority of contemporary Western culture: "We are a wonderful people, and live in a wonderful age. Parachutes and railroads—man-traps and spring guns! Our steamboats are upon every sea, and the Nassau balloon packet is about to run regular trips (fare either way only twenty pounds sterling) between London and Timbuctoo" (T 1:381). Not surprisingly, the General turns out to be a mechanical contrivance himself, an impossible assemblage of manufactured body parts: he had been dismembered ("used up") by the Kickapoo and "Bugaboo" Indians. But it turns out that, in Philadelphia, a used-up man can purchase the finest cork leg from (John F.) Thomas on Race Street, shoulders from the tailor Nicholas Pettitt, a wig from De L'Orme's, teeth from Parmly's, the list goes on.[26] General Smith invokes these names and others—at least some of them real Philadelphia tradesmen—as his "negro valet" assembles him before the narrator's eyes. The story has several satirical angles, as it implicitly criticizes US Indian policy and the unquestioning embrace of technology, but at its heart is another exposure of deceptively respectable appearances. Like Blackwood's political articles, which are actually cut-and-paste plagiarisms, and Peter Pendulum's business methods, which are actually petty swindles, General Smith is an expedient, artificial construction; to the extent that there is a "man" underneath the store-bought prostheses, he is actually "a large and exceedingly odd-looking bundle of something," which the narrator kicks out of the way, not recognizing it as the General. Without commenting directly on Philadelphia's orderly grid and disorderly back alleys, its embrace of industrial progress amid resistance from laborers, Poe, in his first years there, seems to have assumed a cynical distrust of dignified appearances, Franklinian self-assurance, and Quaker probity.

William Burton fired Poe in May 1840. According to his employer, Poe had become unreliable and was planning to launch a competing magazine; according to Poe, Burton was planning to sell the publication without consulting him, leaving him jobless. Poe also claimed that Burton took advantage of authors by advertising premiums—prize contests like the ones Poe had entered while living in Baltimore—then canceling them, but still keeping the entries as unpaid submissions (CL 1:229–30). And it probably didn't help that Poe had borrowed a hundred dollars from Burton (Poe claimed it was only sixty), which Burton had begun garnishing in small amounts from his pay.[27] Meanwhile, Poe *was* planning a new magazine, and Burton *was* planning to sell his, but, even if the two men had been on better terms, Poe did not have the money to purchase a successful magazine with a substantial subscription list. Burton sold *Burton's* in October 1840 to a young, ambitious publisher, George Rex Graham, who combined it with that of another publication, the *Casket*, to create *Graham's Magazine*.

Having lost his position with Burton, Poe immediately began pursuing his professional dream. He circulated a prospectus for his own magazine, whose punning title—the

Penn—evoked his adopted state. Throughout the summer and fall of 1840, he solicited literary contributors and subscribers, using the prospectus as stationery: "THE PENN MAGAZINE, A MONTHLY LITERARY JOURNAL, TO BE EDITED AND PUBLISHED IN THE CITY OF PHILADELPHIA, BY EDGAR A. POE." Poe mentioned his prior connection to the *Southern Literary Messenger* three times but made no reference to *Burton's*. He promised "honest," "fearless" literary criticism, and suggested that literature rather than politics would predominate: "Its aim, chiefly, shall be *to please*; and this through means of versatility, originality and pungency." Poe's magazine would have an elegant, professional look and feel: "the paper will be equal to that of The North American Review [a highly regarded Boston magazine]; the pictorial embellishments will be numerous, and by the leading artists of the country, but will be introduced only in the necessary illustration of the text" (E 1026). Each issue would contain about eighty pages, and the price would be five dollars per year: all of these details signified a high-quality publication. The *Penn* would commence publication in January—the same month *Graham's* was to debut—and, from the notices Poe's project received from friendly publications, including one by Graham himself in the *Saturday Evening Post*, the literati of Philadelphia fully expected it to happen.

But it didn't. A December 29 notice in the *Daily Chronicle*, a paper owned by Poe's friend Charles Alexander, reported that, because of a "severe and continued illness," Poe had been forced to postpone publication until March.[28] Then, on February 4, the unstable economy took another sudden downturn as Nicholas Biddle's US Bank suspended specie payments, setting off a chain reaction throughout Philadelphia and beyond. Two weeks later, George Rex Graham wrote in the *Saturday Evening Post*:

Mr. Poe, we are sorry to say, has been forced, at the last moment, to abandon finally, or at least to postpone indefinitely, his project of the Penn Magazine. This is the more to be regretted as he had the finest prospects of success in the establishment of the journal—such prospects as are seldom enjoyed—an excellent list of subscribers, and, what is equally to the purpose, the universal good-will of the public press. . . . In the present disorder of all monetary affairs, however, it was but common prudence to give up the enterprise—in fact it would have been madness to attempt it. Periodicals are among the principal sufferers by these pecuniary convulsions, and to *commence* one just now would be exceedingly hazardous. It is, beyond doubt, fortunate for Mr. P. that his late illness induced the postponement of his first number; which, it will be remembered, was to have appeared in January.

It is with pleasure we add, that we have secured the services of Mr. Poe as one of the editors of Graham's Magazine.[29]

Graham was right that the timing was prohibitively bad. Poe explained to his friend Thomas Wyatt that he had entered into partnership with a Philadelphia publisher, J. R. Pollack, and that he was "putting the first sheet to press" when the banking crisis struck "like a clap of thunder" (L 1:267). Of course, Graham had launched his own magazine just before the same thunderclap, but he had considerably more capital than Poe, as well as the subscription lists of the *Casket* and *Burton's* to sustain his enterprise.

So it made sense for Poe to swallow his pride and settle for another assistant editor's job with Graham in early 1841. He earned a decent salary of eight hundred dollars per year, with additional pay for literary contributions. Graham knew more about running a magazine than White or Burton, which meant Poe had less editorial control but a more competent and understanding boss. Moreover, Graham seemed to support Poe's goal of establishing the *Penn* when conditions were more favorable, and, as early as June of that year, Poe was writing to a select group of authors, including Washington Irving, James Fenimore Cooper, and Henry Wadsworth Longfellow, whom he hoped would become regular monthly contributors to a magazine that would launch in January 1842 with Graham's financial backing. But this plan never materialized either; Poe was asking for too great a commitment from famous writers who generally had no personal connection to him and were likely put off by the severe, "tomahawking" book reviews that had been his calling card since his days at the *Messenger*.

Poe's $800 salary in 1841 was significantly higher than the $50 per month he had been earning with Burton, and he supplemented it with a little over $200 that year from his writing, primarily for *Graham's*.[30] It was the most he would ever make in a single year. Using the admittedly imprecise measure of the Bureau of Labor Statistics' calculation of average yearly inflation (1.88 percent), Poe's $1,000 would equate with about $27,600 in 2019.[31] To add some perspective, unskilled factory workers made about 63 cents per day in 1841 in Philadelphia, which would amount to less than $200 per year. Carpenters in 1851 earned about $10.50 for a sixty-hour week, probably about $500 per year, so, in 1841, at least, Poe was doing better than most manual laborers.[32] On the other hand, Henry Wadsworth Longfellow, the writer Poe most envied, was making probably three times as much: he was paid an average of about $1,700 per year as a professor of modern languages and belles lettres at Harvard during the same period, supplemented by well over $1,000 per year from poetry and other writing.[33] Although Graham and others were starting to improve the terms of payment for authors, few writers earned enough strictly from book and magazine publications to support a comfortable household, and Poe was not one of those few.[34] By 1840 he had earned enough of a reputation to convince Lea & Blanchard to issue a volume of his first twenty-five stories, *Tales of the Grotesque and Arabesque*, but the publishers saw little chance of the book turning a profit, and offered him no payment other than "a few copies for distribution among your friends." And they were right: no one made money on Poe's collection, which, despite strong reviews, failed to sell its modest print run of 750 copies.[35]

Poe's single biggest payday for a story or poem came from "The Gold-Bug," which in June 1843 won a $100 prize from a Philadelphia weekly, the *Dollar Newspaper*. (Poe had sold the story to Graham for $52, but Graham allowed him to exchange it for "some critical articles" so that he could enter the prize contest.)[36] While the newspaper's title refers to its subscription price, it also provides a fitting gloss on Poe's treasure-seeking story; in fact, the editors seemed especially interested in stories with pecuniary themes, as suggested by the second- and third-place entries, "The Banker's Daughter" and "Marrying for Money."[37] The protagonist of "The Gold-Bug," William Legrand, shrewdly discerns that a piece of seemingly blank parchment is actually a set of coded instructions, written in invisible ink, that lead to a treasure chest buried on a South Carolina barrier island (specifically Sullivan's Island, where Poe had been stationed throughout 1828). With the help of the narrator and a black servant named Jupiter, Legrand unearths the pirate fortune. Poe probably fantasized about an analogous reward for his creative and intellectual skill: significantly, the treasure chest contains "no American money"—at a time when the Bank War had called into question what counted as American money and what any of it was worth—but instead is crammed with diamonds, rubies, emeralds, sapphires, and gold.[38]

The cryptographic plot of "The Gold-Bug" grew out of a journalistic sideshow Poe had operated in the pages of *Alexander's Weekly Messenger* and, later, *Graham's*. Starting with a discussion of "enigmas" and "hieroglyphical writing" in December 1839, Poe vowed to decode any piece of writing that employed the substitution of symbols for letters. He then proceeded to publish the seemingly inscrutable cyphers while bantering with correspondents, professing the ease of cracking their codes. By February 1840 he was already complaining (in the pages of *Alexander's*), "Do people really think that we have nothing in the world to do but to read hieroglyphics?"[39] Poe set up this challenge in a way that would require him to solve only relatively simple cryptograms, but the gimmick still added to his reputation as a kind of intellectual wizard. He had cultivated that image earlier in his career with his exposé of Maelzel's automaton chess player and painstaking literary reviews, and he would soon enhance it further with his detective stories.

Poe's back-and-forth with puzzle enthusiasts was ideal for creating a virtual community of readers in Philadelphia and beyond. Furthermore, his decoding skills would have been particularly associated with city life, which continually presented new phenomena to interpret, and where, according to conventional wisdom, appearances were nearly always deceiving.[40] Poe's friend Lippard would make false appearances the central trope of his blockbuster *The Quaker City* in 1844, and by the mid-1850s the "city mystery" novel, with its focus on the criminal underworld—along with George G. Foster's guidebooks to the hidden pleasures and dangers of the new metropolis (among them *New York by Gaslight* and *Philadelphia in Slices*)—would heighten readers' perception of the city as an agglomeration of signs to be decoded. In these exposés, well-dressed men and women are likely swindlers and prostitutes, oyster bars are fronts for dens of vice, and stately mansions conceal treachery and ill-gotten fortunes.

First published in December 1840, Poe's story "The Man of the Crowd" encapsulates the mystery and fear that attended the rapid development of cities and the influx of "strangers." Though set in London, where Poe had lived as a child and whose density and growth exceeded those of American cities in 1840, the tale reflects the future shock of mid-nineteenth-century urban experience generally. For the first third of the story, the narrator, recuperating from an unnamed illness, sits alone at the "large bow-window" of a coffee house, watching the parade of pedestrians at the workday's end. A shrewd taxonomist of urban types, he identifies the professions and social stations of passersby. The first group includes "noblemen, merchants, attorneys, tradesmen, stock-jobbers . . . men of leisure and men actively engaged in affairs of their own." He proceeds down the social ladder, calling attention to visible clues:

> The tribe of clerks was an obvious one and here I discerned two remarkable divisions. There were the junior clerks of flash houses [pubs that engaged in various illicit activities]—young gentlemen with tight coats, bright boots, well-oiled hair, and supercilious lips. Setting aside a certain dapperness of carriage, which may be termed *deskism* for want of a better word, the manner of these persons seemed to me an exact fac-simile of what had been the perfection of *bon ton* about twelve or eighteen months before. They wore the cast-off graces of the gentry;—and this, I believe, involves the best definition of the class. (T 1:508)

The "upper clerks" are similarly identifiable from appearance, as are "gamblers," "Jew peddlars," "sturdy professional street beggars," "feeble and ghastly invalids," "modest young girls," "women of the town," "drunkards innumerable and indescribable," and, finally, "pie-men, porters, coalheavers, sweeps; organ-grinders, monkey-exhibiters and ballad mongers, those who vended with those who sang; ragged artizans and exhausted laborers of every description, and still all full of a noisy and inordinate vivacity which jarred discordantly upon the ear, and gave an aching sensation to the eye" (T 1:509–10). This extraordinary inventory suggests that the city and its inhabitants, however mysterious to the uninitiated, are decipherable, like a cryptographer's alphabet of arbitrarily selected symbols.

But the narrator eventually spies an enigmatic old man, and feeling "singularly aroused, startled, fascinated," he pursues this "man of the crowd" over the course of an entire night. The list of emotions and dispositions the man suggests to the narrator ("ideas of vast mental power, of caution, of penuriousness, of avarice, of coolness, of malice, of blood-thirstiness, of triumph, of merriment, of excessive terror, of intense—of supreme despair") is so varied, even contradictory, that we might see the man as *embodying* the crowd, somehow reflecting its very diversity, and for that reason escaping the narrator's classification. Indeed, the defining feature of the man's movements throughout the night is his effort to remain *within* a crowd, as if he could exist nowhere else. Literally, the man of the crowd might simply be trying to avoid a solitary encounter with the narrator—another "man of the crowd"—if he realizes he is being followed, but even that precautionary maneuver suggests that the densely populated city is the water he swims in, that he is perfectly acculturated to his environment. In fact, he becomes less at ease whenever the crowd thins. Entering a street "not quite so much thronged as the main one he had quitted," he "walked more slowly and with less object than before—more hesitatingly. He crossed and re-crossed the way repeatedly without apparent aim" (T 1:512). When a bazaar closes for the night and he jostles a shopkeeper closing his shutter, *he* shudders (Poe can't resist the pun), perhaps in fear of having nowhere to go. But then "he hurried into the street, looked anxiously around him for an instant, and then ran with incredible swiftness" before melting into a crowded thoroughfare. If the man is agitated when not in the crowd, he evinces no joy or contentment upon reuniting with the urban throng; he never smiles, and he speaks to no one.

London, the city that Philadelphia and New York in the 1840s may soon become, never sleeps, but the all-nighter it offers "the crowd" isn't much fun. The pursuit of a crowd through the small hours leads the man, and his pursuer, to the slums, described in terms similar to those of the Philadelphia Sanitary Commission quoted earlier. Here "every thing wore the worst impress of the most deplorable poverty, and of the most desperate crime. By the dim light of an accidental lamp, tall, antique, worm-eaten, wooden tenements were seen tottering to their fall" (T 1:514). As night turns to day, the narrator can interpret the man only as "the type and genius of deep crime," although, aside from his possession of a dagger, he exhibits no criminal behavior. His unreadability, ultimately the unreadability of the urban crowd itself, is what terrifies the narrator, who opens the tale with the epigraph "Ce grand Malheur, de ne pouvoir etre seul" and ends it speculating that "it is but one of the great mercies of God that 'er lasst sich nicht lesen.'" The French and German, at least, are translatable—"The great evil, not to be able to be alone," and "it does not permit itself to be read"—but, to the narrator, the untranslatable man of the crowd is not only a mystery but also a horror. Poe seems to have recognized that there was something about the modern city that could not be explicated. Treasure maps could be decoded and cryptographs could be solved, but this coded text remained unreadable. In what could reasonably be called Poe's first detective story, then, the detective fails: if he's looking for a crime, he doesn't find one, and if he is trying to decode the appearance of the man of the crowd, he concludes by admitting, gratefully, that it can't be done.

But, for most fans of the genre, the modern detective story begins not with "The Man of the Crowd" but with Poe's "The Murders in the Rue Morgue," published the following year."[41] As Amy Gilman notes, the detective story is "a form generally associated with urbanization and the development of mass culture," and Poe established that form with "Rue Morgue."[42] Although the city itself is not particularly menacing in this story, it *is* the site of a violent home invasion resulting in the grisly deaths of two innocent women. This time, the seemingly insoluble mystery permits itself to be read by Poe's ingenious detective C. Auguste Dupin, who succeeds largely through an ability to interpret evidence overlooked or misinterpreted by the police. Dupin recognizes that the "murders" in the Rue Morgue are, legally, not murders at all, but the actions of an orangutan that escaped the possession of a sailor.

"Rue Morgue" takes place in Paris, but, as with "The Man of the Crowd," Poe provides few significant local details, while general characteristics of vibrant, rapidly changing cities prove crucial. Again, Poe emphasizes the diversity of urban trades, as the list of witnesses includes a laundress, tobacconist, silversmith, restaurateur, banker, clerk, tailor, undertaker, and confectioner (in addition to the gendarme, physician, and surgeon called to the crime scene). As if to emphasize the anonymity of city life, in the story none of these neighbors really knows the victims, Mme. and Mlle. L'Espanaye, except on business terms. Another sign that the neighborhood is in flux, and becoming more crowded, is the detail that Mme. L'Espanaye had previously leased their house to a jeweler but objected to her tenant's subleasing portions of it: "She became dissatisfied with the abuse of the premises by her tenant, and moved into them herself, refusing to let any portion" (T 1:539). More significant, Dupin comes to realize that the culprit might not be human because, in their depositions, neighbors who hear the incident disagree as to which language the intruder with the "shrill" voice is speaking. In this multicultural environment, the witnesses themselves speak different languages, and they consistently report hearing a language they do not understand. In each case, the supposed language is one that might plausibly be heard in a Paris neighborhood: the French witnesses identify the "language" as Spanish or Italian, the Dutchman believes it is French, and the Englishman hears German.[43]

But, of course, the voice, and the violence, come from an orangutan, which provides "Rue Morgue" with a distinctly Philadelphian context. In the summer of 1839, the Masonic Hall on Chestnut Street exhibited a female chimpanzee, which was erroneously referred to as an "ourang outang" in the press. The advertisement in the *Philadelphia Gazette* described the animal as "lately brought from Africa," the genuine 'Troglodytes Niger' of Naturalists, or 'Wild Man of the Woods.' . . . It bears a most striking resemblance to the human form, and in natural sagacity far exceeds the description of Naturalists." The *Pennsylvania Inquirer* affirmed the advertisement's claim, calling the orangutan "in all probability the nearest approach of any animal to the human form." Poe's friend John DuSolle was more specific, writing in the *Spirit of the Times* that "the color of the skin, when examined closely, is seen to be that of a bright mulatto. She evinces a degree of intelligence but little behind that of the human species, which in appearance and actions she so much resembles."[44] Poe would certainly have been aware of the exhibit, which, bolstered by newspapers and magazines, seems to have created a sensation. He would have also known of, and perhaps attended, a performance advertised in the *Gazette* the following April, by Signor Hervio Nano, a "dwarf" actor, in the role of "Bibboo, the Island Ape, or Ourang Outang," in a play called *The Shipwreck*. Elsewhere, the *Gazette* promised that Nano's "strength and agility, notwithstanding his peculiarities of figure, are very extraordinary, and his feats, especially as the ape, are of a surprising character."[45]

As the publicity for those exhibitions suggests, nineteenth-century Americans' fascination with apes had much to do with their seemingly uncanny resemblance to humans and their place in the primate hierarchy that included racial divisions. Calling African orangutans (or chimpanzees) "wild men of the woods" and likening their skin color to "mulattos" invoked a well-established racist comparison of African people—and their American descendants—to apes.[46] Almost certainly, Poe's contemporaries would have made that association while reading "Rue Morgue," whether consciously "interpreting" the story as racially coded or not.[47] Literary scholar Elise Lemire situates the story's use of an orangutan within two phenomena specific (though not exclusive) to antebellum Philadelphia: the prevalence of black barbers in the city and fears of race mixing or "amalgamation." The barbering profession was a highly visible vehicle of economic advancement for African Americans in Philadelphia in the 1830s and 1840s, engaging about 5 percent of the total black workforce by mid-century.[48] The black barber became a stereotype, sometimes a humiliating one: for instance, Lemire notes that, in the 1830s, the stuffed monkeys in Peale's museum in Philadelphia were depicted as barbers, posed as if shaving each other with razors.[49]

And, because of African Americans' success as barbers, the stereotype tended to ridicule their supposed pretentious and inappropriate social climbing, which in the mind of most whites was never far from the threat of sexual race mixing. Indeed, the riot that destroyed Pennsylvania Hall in 1838 had been fueled by those fears; a lithograph titled *The Evening Before the Conflagration* represented the hall as an "interracial brothel."[50] Poe's use of a razor-wielding orangutan, imported from Borneo, who escapes from a white master, enters the abode of two white women, and ultimately kills them, clearly invokes a set of racist associations set in place by the time of the story's publication. Poe had no apparent reason to stoke racial resentment and violence, and, having read the story many times, I find it hard to imagine that he wrote it with that explicit motive. At the same time, he clearly didn't mind using the racist tropes that were already in circulation, and that, he well knew, provided a pretext for real violence on the streets of Philadelphia.

Decoding cryptographs, inventing the literary detective, and writing a handful of the most enduring gothic tales in the English language, Poe continued an incredible creative streak that began almost as soon as he arrived in Philadelphia. Moreover, while working for *Graham's* in 1841–42, he was at the helm of one of the most widely circulated magazines in the country. If he was not one of the most famous literary figures in America, he was becoming better known, and he had developed a strong reputation for his intellect and versatility. His friend Jesse Dow proclaimed in the Philadelphia paper the *Index*, "Mr. Poe is a wonderful man. He can read the hieroglyphics of the Pharoahs, tell you what you are thinking about while he walks beside you, and criticise you into shape without giving offence."[51] When Dickens visited Philadelphia during his highly publicized US tour in March 1842, Poe was granted a private meeting, possibly

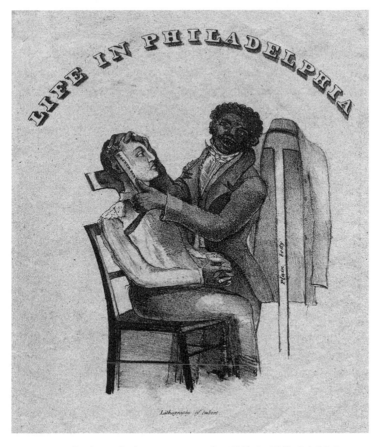

Figure 3.4 Anthony Imbert, wrapper for "Life in Philadelphia" cartoons, ca. 1830. Many of the single-panel cartoons (created by E. W. Clay) were racist caricatures of African Americans. (Historical Society of Pennsylvania Digital Library.)

two sessions, at Dickens's hotel. (Poe asked Dickens for his help in securing a British publisher for his tales; Dickens politely assented but seems to have made only a half-hearted effort to fulfill the promise.)

Despite the stability and renown that came from his work at *Graham's*, Poe left the magazine in the spring of 1842, perhaps a few weeks after his meeting with Dickens. He had held the job for just over a year, approximately the same duration as his employment with the *Messenger* and *Burton*'s. But this separation seems to have been far more amicable than his breaks with White and Burton, and the evidence suggests that Poe, not Graham, instigated it.[52] Poe had certainly contributed to the magazine's impressive growth—having started with a circulation of 5,500 less than two years earlier, Graham boasted of printing 40,000 copies in March 1842, just months before Poe's departure—but it was Graham who was getting rich from the enterprise, while Poe's dream of his own magazine was repeatedly deferred.[53] He told Frederick Thomas in May 1842, "My reason for resigning was disgust with the namby-pamby character of the Magazine—a character which it was impossible to eradicate—I allude to the contemptible pictures, fashion-plates, music and love tales. The salary, moreover, did not pay me for the labor which I was forced to bestow. With Graham who is really a very gentlemanly, although an exceedingly weak man, I had no misunderstanding" (L 1:333).

Though he did continue to sell stories, to Graham and others, at a steady pace, Poe could not replace even the modest income he derived from editing *Graham's*. His earnings for the remainder of his time in Philadelphia would place him below the poverty line. Meanwhile, his successor at the magazine, Rufus W. Griswold, would receive a thousand-dollar salary, two hundred dollars more than Poe's. Griswold, a twenty-seven-year-old editor who had recently worked for Horace Greeley's *New York Tribune*, would soon become known as a leading anthologist of American writing. The year before joining *Graham's*, Griswold had edited *The Poets and Poetry of America*, which included three poems by Poe—a rather slight representation. According to Poe, Griswold bribed him to write a positive review of the book; perhaps as revenge for his underrepresentation, Poe delivered a less-than-bribe-worthy product, complimenting but also insulting the volume's editor. It marked the beginning of a rivalry, sometimes masked in friendship, that would continue, infamously, even after Poe's death.

Poe's decision to leave *Graham's* followed closely upon a harrowing development in his personal life: Virginia had contracted tuberculosis. One evening in early 1842, while singing at home, she began coughing up blood. Virginia was only nineteen years old; with this incident, she went from a prolonged childhood, petted and protected by Edgar and Muddy, to a condition in which she would again be treated much like a child. The best evidence that she and Edgar enjoyed some brief period of mature romantic love between those phases comes from a story he wrote in 1841, when Virginia still appeared healthy. "Eleonora" presents a fairy-tale version of Poe's household: the narrator, named Pyrros in the first version, his cousin Eleonora, and her mother form a world unto themselves in a "Valley of the Many-Colored Grass." When Eleonora is fifteen and Pyrros twenty (shrinking the age difference between Edgar and Virginia), they fall in love. At that moment, their physical world comes to reflect the change, implicitly sexual, in their relationship:

> The passions which had for centuries distinguished our race came thronging with the fancies for which they had been equally noted, and together breathed a delirious bliss over the Valley of the Many-Colored Grass. A change fell upon all things. Strange brilliant flowers, star-shaped, burst out upon the trees where no flowers had been known before. The tints of the green carpet deepened; and when, one by one, the white daisies shrank away, there sprang up, in place of them, ten by ten of the ruby-red asphodel. (T 1:640)

Then Eleonora becomes fatally ill, and Pyrros pledges that his faithfulness will endure after her death. She promises to watch over him, and to return to him visibly or at least "give me frequent indications of her presence" (T 1:642). After she dies, they both stay true to their words, until Pyrros falls hopelessly in love with another woman, Ermengarde. Poe had written other stories ("Morella," "Ligeia," "The Fall of the House of Usher") about women who die and come back, and they do not come back to *comfort* the men who bury them. But Eleonora gives her blessing to Pyrros: "'Sleep in peace!—for the Spirit of Love reigneth and ruleth, and, in taking to thy passionate heart her who is Ermengarde, thou art absolved, for reasons which shall be made known to thee in Heaven, of thy vows unto Eleonora" (T 1:645). The implication of the phrase "reasons which shall be made known to thee in Heaven" is that Ermengarde *is* Eleonora. Possibly Poe knew or suspected that Virginia was ill before the singing incident; otherwise, "Eleonora" is eerily prophetic of her sickness and death, Poe's subsequent need to find another wife, and the guilt that would accompany that quest. If read autobiographically, the story also suggests that there was, perhaps, a happy, brief interval in Edgar and Virginia's marriage between her childhood and her invalidism—or that Poe dearly wished there had been. Virginia's health would fluctuate over the next five years, as she endured extended bouts of fatigue, coughing, and chills.

Although the family lived in the less crowded western portion of Philadelphia, they must have had reason to believe the northern suburbs would be healthier for Virginia than the city proper. Or perhaps they were just seeking cheaper rent. But not long after her illness became apparent, and around the same time Poe left *Graham's*, the family moved from the "old place" near Rittenhouse Square. They might have stayed temporarily in a boardinghouse, location unknown, but by September 1842 they had settled into what is now the Fairmount district at the corner of Twenty-Fifth and Coates Street (Fairmount Avenue) near the waterworks (within a few blocks of what is now the Philadelphia Museum of Art). This location put Poe farther from the publishing center—about two and a half miles—but, no longer working at *Graham's*, he would not have had to make the trek as frequently. Frederick W. Thomas, who visited Poe there in September 1842, described it as "a rural home on the outskirts of the city. . . . [S]mall, but comfortable inside for one of the kind. The rooms looked neat and orderly, but everything about the place wore an air of pecuniary want."[54]

A later reminiscence by John S. Detwiler, who as a boy had been Poe's next-door neighbor, identifies their landlord as Michel Bouvier, a prominent cabinetmaker and importer of marble and mahogany (and great-great-grandfather of Jacqueline Kennedy Onassis). Detwiler also recalls hunting birds with his older friend: "When Poe asked me to go with him and reed birds I went. . . . We got into a boat and paddled down to Gray's Ferry [2–3 miles south on the Schuylkill]. I rowed while he loaded and shot. For many of the birds I waded in water up to my chin. We brought home a big bag."[55] Close to the river and far from the city center, the Fairmount district was nonetheless well traveled and hardly undeveloped: a (horse-drawn) railroad ran directly behind Poe's house; breweries and iron foundries were among the industries moving into the area. The family lived within a few blocks of the city hospital for contagious diseases, the Great Western Hotel, and Eastern State Penitentiary.[56] This "modern" prison made solitary confinement and silence the norm for inmates, on the theory that solitude and reflection would induce penitence. The imposing structure, which still stands, featured a neo-gothic exterior and a widely imitated hub-and-spoke design to make it easier to

Figure 3.5 Eastern State Penitentiary, a new "model" prison located about two blocks from Poe's residence for about half a year, 1842–43.

monitor cellblocks. In its long shadow, Poe wrote two classic confession narratives, written or voiced from prison cells: "The Tell-Tale Heart" and "The Black Cat," both composed in late 1842. In fact, the latter story might have been inspired by a news item reprinted in a Philadelphia paper about the bones of a murdered woman discovered in a cellar in Greenfield, Connecticut.[57] Poe had recently completed another story, "The Pit and the Pendulum," set in Spain during the Inquisition but evocative of the new model prison, with its emphasis on isolation and the subjection of prisoners to constant surveillance.[58] "My every motion," recalls Poe's imprisoned narrator, "was undoubtedly watched" (T 1:695).

In late spring 1843, Poe, Virginia, and Maria moved about two miles east and slightly south, to the area known as Spring Garden. Philadelphia historian Ellis Oberholtzer describes the expanding suburb's situation at the time: "Some six squares (from town) along a well-traveled highway leading into the centre of the city, a locality of market commerce, but where a number of well-to-do Quaker families had their homes."[59] While still semirural, the new location was closer to the commercial and publishing center, where Poe—or Maria, his sometime emissary—still had literary business to conduct.[60] Here, too, one might presume that rent played a role in the decision: although there is no record of his being evicted from the Coates Street house, Poe must have struggled to pay the rent and probably fell behind. The new home, on North Seventh Street just above Spring Garden Street, was owned by a successful plumber named William Alburger. According to Alburger's daughter and another neighbor, the Poes were always behind on rent, but the new landlord "was not disposed to cause him distress."[61]

The Spring Garden house, now the Edgar Allan Poe National Historic Site, must have seemed luxuriously large for the small family: three stories, six rooms, plus a cellar.[62] The most detailed description when Poe lived there is a somewhat unreliable account of Thomas Mayne Reid, a writer of adventure novels who spent time with Poe in Philadelphia. Writing approximately twenty-five years after the fact, Reid recalled the house as "a lean-to of three rooms, (there may have been a garret with a closet,) of painted plank construction, supported against the gable of the more pretentious dwelling"; elsewhere he referred to it as a "'shanty' supported against the gable of the rich Quaker,"

Figure 3.6 Poe, Virginia, and Maria lived in the smaller attached house on North Seventh Street. This house in Spring Garden was their last residence in Philadelphia before they moved to New York City.

stressing the contrast between Poe's poverty and his landlord's wealth.[63] Since Reid was writing to defend Poe's posthumous reputation, he might have thought the contrast would highlight the injustice of Poe's (very real) poverty—or he might have simply misremembered (he also thought Poe's Quaker landlord was a cereal maker). The term "lean-to" might technically apply, since the building Poe and family lived in was constructed against the larger house, with a slanted roof attached to a wall, but the rest of the description, in particular the word "shanty," will strike any visitor to the National Historic Site as misleading. At some point the family acquired some decent furniture, including a horsehair sofa and "prized red carpet," which they eventually left with Alburger in lieu of back rent.[64]

The onset of Virginia's illness and Poe's departure from *Graham's* not only led to the family's move from the "old place" to the northern suburbs; the disruption also spawned frequent episodes of drunkenness, after a long period of relative sobriety. Genetically predisposed to alcoholism and low alcohol tolerance, Poe wasn't helped in having come of age at a time when men typically drank throughout the day, every day, and by living in cities with drinking establishments on nearly every block. Per capita alcohol consumption in the United States seems to have peaked around 1830, when Poe was twenty-one.[65] And there were over nine hundred taverns in Philadelphia in 1841, including one run by C. W. House a block away from Poe's Spring Garden abode.[66] Meanwhile, the temperance movement was changing attitudes toward drinking, reducing alcohol sales dramatically by the 1840s. The movement's success also meant that there were now many men and women making a point of abstaining and seeking to reform others, which is probably one reason reports of Poe's drinking appear as often as they do in the documentary record. Poe's sober contemporaries were not likely to dismiss or normalize his drinking problem, nor were they likely to regard it as an illness, but as a character flaw. For example, when Poe's employer William Burton opened his own theater in 1840, he took the principled step of banning the sale of alcohol on the premises; not surprisingly, Burton clashed with Poe over his drinking and publicly referred to his former editor's "infirmities" in apologizing for a subscription error in his magazine.[67] Thomas Dunn English, another teetotaler, had been Poe's friend when he worked for *Burton's*, but when the two men had a falling out, largely as a result of an alcohol-fueled insult, English broadcast Poe's drinking problem through a thinly veiled caricature in his novel *The Doom of the Drinker*, serialized in the *Cold Water Magazine* in 1843. This is not to say that Burton or English exaggerated Poe's drinking problem; rather, that, as temperance men, they judged him for it and had no compunction about publicly shaming him.

In reminiscences published long after Poe's death, English elaborated on his history with Poe, corroborating other claims that Poe managed to stay sober for significant periods of time ("His offenses against sobriety were committed at irregular intervals") but was incapable of drinking moderately ("He had not that physical constitution which would permit him to be a regular drinker").[68] English recalled one occasion when he found Poe "struggling in a vain attempt to raise himself from the gutter." He guided his staggering companion home:

> The house stood back, and was only a part of a house. They had a habit at that time in Philadelphia of building houses so that there was a stairway between dining room and kitchen back, and the parlor in front. The owner of this house had only built the rear portion, and the ground where the front was to stand in future had been turned into a grassplot, with a flower border against the adjoining brick wall. I knocked at the door, and Mrs. Clemm opened it. Raising her voice, she cried, "You make Eddie drunk, and then you bring him home." As I was turning away Poe grasped me by the shoulder and said: "Never mind the old——; come in."
>
> I shook myself from his clutch and, merely telling Mrs. Clemm that if I found Eddie in the gutter again I'd leave him there, went on my way.
>
> Three days after when I saw Poe—for if I remember rightly the next two days he was not at the office—he was

heartily ashamed of the matter, and said that it was an unusual thing with him, and would never occur again.[69]

If English's remarkably detailed account is accurate, the incident probably occurred at "the old place," since he situates it during Poe's self-proclaimed sober period, when he
worked for Burton—in which case, it provides at least a
little information about the house near Sixteenth and Locust. But it is also noteworthy for the disdain English expressed, half a century after the fact, toward drunken Edgar,
as well as Maria's insinuation that he, English, was a drinking companion.

The cost of alcoholism to Poe's social life and career were
enormous. Knowing that he should abstain altogether, Poe
probably felt trapped by invitations to have a drink: he could
either appear antisocial by declining or become truly antisocial by drinking to excess. He probably did not drink at home;
in fact, being away from home for an extended time increased
the likelihood of an embarrassing episode. In the summer of
1842, during the crisis period following Virginia's first hem-
orrhage, Poe traveled to New York looking for work, probably contemplating a relocation of cities after leaving the
"old place" near Rittenhouse Square. He became intoxicated,
apparently for several days, and was eventually found in the
woods near Jersey City, "wandering about like a crazy man,"
according to his former girlfriend Mary Starr, who saw him
on that trip.[70] In March 1843, Poe made a week-long trip
to Washington, DC, to solicit subscriptions and contributions
for his prospective magazine, now called the *Stylus*—and,
more important, to try to attain a government appointment
with the help of Frederick Thomas, who was a friend of
President John Tyler's son Robert. But Thomas fell ill and was
unavailable as a guide; Poe made the rounds with his friend
Jesse Dow, but he began drinking and behaving badly. Dow

reported back to Thomas Clarke, Poe's business partner for the *Stylus*, that Poe had become "quite unreliable" and that he "exposes himself here to those who may injure him very much with the President."[71] Among the men Poe insulted in Washington was none other than Thomas Dunn English. Not only did Poe not get the clerkship he sought, but in the aftermath of the Washington episode he also lost the financial support of Clarke, who, like English, was a temperance advocate.[72] Poe's drinking and (consequent) erratic behavior might not have been the sole cause, but it seems to have troubled Clarke; in any case, the breakup of the short-lived partnership of Clarke & Poe (as their names appeared on the prospectus) dashed Poe's renewed hopes for establishing a Philadelphia-based magazine.[73]

Poe stayed in Spring Garden for another year after the Washington debacle, contributing literary criticism to *Graham's* and writing new stories. The success of "The Gold-Bug" in the summer of 1843 provided a financial boost and some measure of fame; the story was even adapted for stage performance at the Walnut Street Theatre on August 8, a "farewell benefit" for the actor-playwright Silas S. Steele, with another popular performer, J. H. "Coal" White, performing the part of Jupiter in blackface.[74] Meanwhile, the story itself became a local controversy that summer, as suspicions were aired about the contest having been rigged and the story plagiarized.[75] At this point, Poe didn't need any bad press, with friends in the Philadelphia publishing world expressing concern and frustration with him privately. Lambert Wilmer, a longtime Poe associate, wrote to a mutual friend that Poe "has become one of the strangest of our literati. He and I are old friends,——have known each other since boyhood, and it gives me inexpressible pain to notice the vagaries to which he has lately become subject. Poor fellow! He is no teetotaler by any means, and I fear he is going headlong to destruction, moral, physical and intellectual."[76] In early 1844, George Graham, who remained on nominally good terms with Poe, complained to Henry Wadsworth Longfellow, promising not to print a "savage" review that Poe had written of Longfellow's latest book: "I do not know what your crime may be in the eyes of Poe, but suppose it may be a better, and more widely established reputation. Or if you have wealth . . . that is sufficient to settle your damnation so far as Mr Poe may be presumed capable of effecting it." Graham clearly felt this sort of resentment from Poe himself, as he proceeded to tell Longfellow that he recently loaned Poe some money, then learned that within an hour Poe "abused" him to another acquaintance "as an exclusive" (that is, a snob).[77]

Poe moved the family from Philadelphia to New York in April 1844. Many years later, T. D. English suggested that there was a specific, disreputable cause for Poe's departure: "I am the sole possessor of this scandalous secret, and as its recital would do no good to any one, the whole affair shall be buried with me." There might have been a scandalous explanation for Poe's departure from Philadelphia, but none is necessary. Poe wasn't making enough money, he was drinking too much, and he was alienating his friends; he needed a new start in a new environment, a city with prospects for steady income. Down but not out in the months before leaving Philadelphia, he began lecturing on American poetry, capitalizing on the popularity of Rufus Griswold's *Poets and Poetry of America* while taking the opportunity to criticize it. He spoke to an overflow crowd at the Juliana Street Church, not far from his Spring Garden home, on November 21, 1843; a week later at Temperance Hall (ironically enough) in Wilmington, Delaware; on December 23 at Newark Academy in Delaware; at the Philadelphia Museum on January 10; and in Baltimore on January 31.[78]

Figure 3.7 Walnut Street Theatre, where a production of "The Gold-Bug" was staged on August 8, 1843. Archival image blended with contemporary photograph. (Archival image: Cooper Hewitt, Smithsonian Design Museum / Art Resource, NY.)

His six years in Philadelphia had not radically changed Poe, but they had advanced his career significantly as an editor, critic, and cryptographer, while giving rise to his full development as a writer of tales. Though his identity had largely been formed in Richmond, Poe was no southern stranger in a strange northern land: he adopted Philadelphia for as long as he lived there, made friends and enemies, and generally immersed himself in the city's print and periodical culture. At the same time, he responded, mostly in fiction, to some of the mid-nineteenth-century city's defining characteristics: alienation, ethnic diversity, racial tension, and the inscrutability of the urban landscape and its inhabitants.

CHAPTER 4

New York (1844–1848)

My dear Muddy,
  We have just this minute done breakfast, and I now sit
    down to write you about everything.

So began Poe's first letter from New York City, written on April 7, 1844: a buoyant, detailed update to Maria Clemm, who would soon join him and Virginia there. He rhapsodized over the bounteous feasts presented to them at their boarding house: "Last night, for supper, we had the nicest tea you ever drank, strong & hot—wheat bread & rye bread—cheese—tea-cakes (elegant) a great dish (2 dishes) of elegant ham, and 2 of cold veal, piled up like a mountain and large slices—3 dishes of the cakes, and every thing in the greatest profusion. No fear of starving here." Unless he ran out of money, of course. There are eight references to prices, buying, and borrowing in this relatively brief letter, suggesting that there *may* have been fear of starving in Philadelphia, a likely motivation for moving to New York. Clearly, Poe was seeking a fresh start, and the decision to relocate was a calculated gamble that he believed would pay off if he could remain frugal and sober: "We have now got 4 $ and half left. Tomorrow I am going to try & borrow 3 $—so that I may have a fortnight to go upon. I feel in excellent spirits & have'nt drank a drop—so that I hope so[on] to get out of trouble" (L 1:437–38). He *would* get out of trouble in New York, and then get into more trouble, following his lifelong pattern of self-sabotage. Poe would be most productive and stable when he was able to live in a rural setting outside the city, and most self-destructive when living in densely populated lower Manhattan. But lower Manhattan—specifically, the district just south of city hall, radiating from the intersection of Nassau and Fulton Streets—was the world he had come to conquer, and much of his writing over the next few years would comment directly or indirectly on his experience there.

New York's rise as the nation's economic and cultural capital is one of the most dramatic developments of the antebellum period. Having established itself as the national financial center in the wake of the American Revolution, the city saw unparalleled economic growth after 1825, when the opening of the Erie Canal made it the hub of commercial traffic.[1] Meanwhile, largely as a result of German and Irish immigration, the city's population—at a time when "the city" referred only to Manhattan—soared from 123,706 in 1820 to 312,710 in 1840 to 813,669 in 1860.[2] Consequently, Lower Manhattan became increasingly crowded while the urban frontier moved rapidly northward, despite the temporary slowdown caused by the Panic of 1837. Less than 10 percent of the population resided above Fourteenth Street in the early 1830s, but by the end of the 1850s more than 50 percent would. Developers snatched up available land, building on what had previously been green space and creating no new parks (until Central Park was established in 1857) as the grid expanded.[3] Fire and water—specifically the Great Fire of December 1835 and the construction of the Croton Waterworks, which began in 1837—changed the physical and social landscape as well. The fire and subsequent rebuilding frenzy "touched off a pell-mell flight of the wealthy" northward, according to historians Edwin G. Burrows and Mike Wallace.[4] The new mansions were the first to be outfitted for running water, provided by the system of aqueducts, tunnels, and pipes from the Croton River.[5] The introduction of north-south rail transportation in 1831, combined with ever-increasing omnibus traffic, sped up the pace of city life and made simply crossing the street an adventure.[6]

Both foreign and domestic observers of antebellum New York were amazed at the chaotic energy and acceleration of change. Fanny Kemble described the city in her journal (published in 1835) as "an irregular collection of temporary buildings, erected for some casual purpose, full of life, animation, and variety, but not meant to endure for any length of time."[7] As for the buildings that did endure, their use was likely to change with the city's demographics. "He who erects his magnificent palace on Fifth Avenue to-day," predicted the philosopher Henry Philip Tappan, "has only fitted out a future boarding-house, and probably occupied the site of a future warehouse."[8] Writing in 1845, former mayor Philip Hone concurred: "Overturn, overturn, overturn! is the maxim of New York. . . . The very bones of our ancestors are not permitted to lie quiet a quarter of a century, and one generation of men seem studious to remove all relics of those who precede them."[9] May 1, the annual "moving day," when leases turned over and tenants flooded the streets with all their belongings, seemed to epitomize Gotham; the very fact that such a large percentage of the city's inhabitants lived in boardinghouses signified a population conditioned to transience.[10] In the words of Lady Emmeline Stuart-Wortley in 1849, "Nothing and nobody seem to stand still for half a moment in New York."[11] A renter like most New Yorkers, Poe had at least five different residences in Manhattan between his arrival in April 1844 and his removal to Fordham in mid-1846. Having spent most of his time in Philadelphia living on the outskirts or in nascent suburbs, he probably found the bustling, crowded

Figure 4.1 Unknown artist, *Moving Day in Little Old New York*, ca. 1827. Poe experienced the pandemonium associated with Moving Day (May 1) and wrote about it in his journalistic series *Doings of Gotham*. (Bequest of Mrs. Screven Lorillard [Alice Whitney] from the collection of Mrs. J. Insley Blair, 2016. The Metropolitan Museum of Art, New York, New York.)

streets and ever-changing landscape of lower Manhattan unnerving.

But Poe must have felt that New York was where he needed to be at this point in his career. Despite his success as an editor and a fiction writer in Philadelphia, after parting with George Graham and discovering Virginia's tuberculosis, his life there had become increasingly unstable, professionally and personally. His plan to establish his own magazine had been deferred too many times to be viable in Philadelphia, where he no longer had the promise of Graham's financial backing. The letter that opens this chapter suggests that he believed that the change of cities would help him turn a corner toward prosperity and sobriety. He already had one steady, if not exactly high-profile, assignment lined up as the "New York Correspondent" for a Pennsylvania paper, and he was sufficiently well known as a "magazinist" that he could expect to find editorial or freelance work. Most of all, it was probably the city's gravitational pull as a publishing mecca that drew Poe in.

Almost immediately, he tested the waters of New York's sea of print with what became known as the "Balloon Hoax." A week after Poe wrote his effusive letter to Muddy describing boardinghouse delicacies, he published an account in the daily New York *Sun* of a transatlantic balloon voyage, under the headline "Astounding News by Express, via Norfolk! The Atlantic Crossed in Three Days, Signal Triumph of Mr. Monck Mason's Flying Machine! Arrival at Sullivan's Island, near Charleston, S. C.—After a Passage of Seventy-Five Hours, etc." Of course, this voyage had not taken place; no one would even attempt a transatlantic balloon voyage for another fifteen years, and no one would succeed until 1978. However, Monck Mason (a real person) *had* successfully piloted a balloon from London to Weilburg, Germany, and published an account of it seven years earlier. Drawing heavily from Mason's account, Poe made his hoax as plausible as possible, incorporating technical details from that voyage and presenting part of the story as a journal kept by the aeronauts.[12] Judging from the responses of other papers, few people were taken in—in this regard, it didn't help that the *Sun* had published a moon-voyage hoax several years earlier—but Poe later insisted that he had created a sensation, writing that "I never witnessed more intense excitement to get possession of the newspaper" (D 33).

Poe also tried his hand at a popular form of journalism with "Doings of Gotham," written for a small-town Pennsylvania weekly, the *Columbia Spy*. By 1844, serialized informal reports or "letters" from the metropolis had become

Figure 4.2 Soon after his arrival in New York City in 1844, Poe created a hoax describing a transatlantic balloon voyage for the *Sun* newspaper. (Harry Ransom Center, Digital Collections, the University of Texas at Austin.)

a thriving subgenre, as New York's transformation fascinated both its own inhabitants and readers throughout the United States. By the early 1840s, a variety of periodicals—from the *Charleston Mercury* to the *Cincinnati Gazette* to the *New England Weekly Review*—featured first-person dispatches from New York (though the writers were frequently anonymous) that described personal encounters with the hustle and flow of big city life.[13] In February 1844, the *New York Herald* griped about the trendiness of the form:

"It seems that the various leading papers, in many of the States and large cities throughout the Union, do not think their newspaper arrangements complete, unless they have a 'New York correspondent,' who furnishes them with the fiddle-faddle, chit-chat-, and other small balderdash, which can be picked up on Broadway, at the bar-rooms, lobbies of the theatres, and other places of public resort in this Babylon."[14]

In using the phrase "chit-chat," the *Herald* invoked one of the most popular magazinists of the time: Nathaniel Parker Willis, whose series "Chit-Chat of New York" was running in the *National Intelligencer* of Washington, DC, as well as the local *New Mirror* (which he edited) in 1844. Willis wrote additional series entitled "Sketches of the Metropolis" and "Daguerreotype Sketches of New York," the latter aiming to provide with words the visual clarity and precision of the newly popular photographic process. Willis's style was gossipy, playful, and—true to his daguerreotype metaphor—highly descriptive.[15] Venturing into the "New York Letters" genre, Poe seems to have modeled his persona initially on Willis, who would soon be his employer at the *Mirror*.[16] Though the resemblance fades over the course of "Doings of Gotham," in the first letter Poe is clearly imitating Willis's breezy style of journalism:

> It will give me much pleasure, gentlemen, to comply with your suggestions and, by dint of a weekly epistle, keep you *au fait* to a certain portion of the doings of Gotham. And here if, in the beginning, for "certain," you read "*uncertain*," you will the more readily arrive at my design. For, in fact, I must deal chiefly in gossip—in gossip, whose empire is unlimited, whose influence is universal, whose devotees are legion;—in gossip, which is the true safety-valve of society—engrossing at least seven-eighths of the whole waking existence of mankind. (D 23)

The emphasis on gossip, the elevated language ("epistle"; "*au fait*"), and the rhetorical apology for his own lack of serious purpose all evoke Willis's trademark persona: a loquacious, cosmopolitan dandy.

Poe was either unable or unwilling to sustain the effervescent tone, but over seven installments he mixed random notes on the literary and publishing scene with other "doings" around town. When not commenting on literary New York, he discussed miscellaneous topics including footraces, peep shows, architecture, political campaigns, blue laws (he was against them), the latest telescope, the presidential election, and an expedition to the South Pole. Having just moved from Philadelphia, Poe made occasional references to his recent home, but he neither declared nor implied any moral judgment about New York through these comparisons, other than to point out that Gotham was generally dirtier than its rival to the south. Poe joined the chorus of commentators on the rapid pace, and particularly the pace of *change*, in New York:

A day or two [ago] I procured a light skiff, and with the aid of a pair of sculls, (as they here term short oars, or paddles) made my way around Blackwell's [now Roosevelt] Island, on a voyage of discovery and exploration. The chief interest of the adventure lay in the scenery of the Manhattan shore, which is here particularly picturesque. The houses are, without exception, frame, and antique. Nothing very modern has been attempted—a necessary result of the subdivision of the whole island into streets and town-lots. I could not look on the magnificent cliffs, and stately trees, which at every moment met my view, without a sigh for their inevitable doom—inevitable and swift. In twenty years, or thirty at farthest, we shall see here nothing more romantic than shipping, warehouses, and wharves. (D 40–41)

When twenty-first-century readers imagine Poe, he's usually not paddling on the East River contemplating the transformation of his physical environment. And yet he probably did make this trip, and, in any case, he was comfortable adopting the persona of someone who did. Poe seems to have known that this sort of excursion, these sentimental observations—on the changing cityscape, the destruction of anything old—were generic conventions of the "New York Correspondence."

"The city is thronged with strangers," Poe wrote in his second letter, "and everything wears an aspect of intense life" (D 31). Poe likely moved house on May 1, experiencing firsthand the day's notorious chaos, to which he alluded in his first letter: "We are not yet over the bustle of the first of May. 'Keep Moving' have been the watchwords for the last fortnight. The man who, in New York, would be so bold as not to peregrinate on the first, would, beyond doubt, attain immortality as 'The Great Unmoved'—a title applied by Horne, the author of 'Orion,' to one of his heroes, Akinetos, the type of the spirit of Apathy" (D 24). Not surprisingly, Poe sympathized with the mythical "Great Unmoved" amid the constant motion of New York. He also praised the "unspoiled" parts of the city—foreshadowing Whitman, he referred to it by the indigenous American name "Manahatta"—and disapproved of "improvement." He described the "shanties of the Irish squatters" as "picturesque" and lamented the impending doom of old wooden mansions: "The spirit of Improvement has withered them with its acrid breath," he wrote. "Streets are already 'mapped' through them, and they are no longer suburban residences, but 'town-lots.'" Elsewhere he complained that "in some thirty years every noble cliff will be a pier, and the whole island will be densely desecrated by buildings of brick, with portentous *facades* of brown-stone, or brown-*stonn*, as the Gothamites have it" (D 26).

Poe was particularly distressed by new architectural developments in Brooklyn (not yet incorporated into New York City), which he described in his fifth letter. "I know few towns which inspire me with so great disgust and contempt," he wrote, mainly because of the new style of houses being built there: "What can be more silly and pitiably absurd than palaces of painted white pine, fifteen feet by twenty?" (D 59) In his earlier story "The Business Man," one of Peter Proffitt's scams was to build shanties next to fashionable new palaces, enticing his neighbor to pay him to move his "eyesore"; the Poe of "Doings of Gotham" clearly preferred the "eyesore," as he condemned the architects of "Brooklynite 'villa's'" to hell: "I really can see little difference between putting up such a house as this, and blowing up a House of Parliament, or cutting the throat of one's grandfather" (D 60).[17] He was not terribly enamored of Brooklyn's street vendors, either. They made life noisy, as did inferior stone pavement—although for that problem, Poe had a solution:

Of the stereatomic wooden pavement, we hear nothing, now, at all. The people seem to have given it up altogether—but nothing better could be invented. We inserted the blocks, without preparation, and they failed. Therefore, we abandoned the experiment. Had they been Kyanized [that is, chemically treated], the result would have been very different, and the wooden causeways would have been in extensive use throughout the country. . . . In point of cheapness, freedom from noise, ease of cleaning, pleasantness to the hoof, and, finally, in point of durability, there is *no* equal to that of the Kyanized wood. But it will take us, as usual, fully ten years to make this discovery. In the meantime, the present experiments with unprepared wood will answer very well for the profit of the street-menders, and for the amusement of common-councils—who will, perhaps, in the next instance, experiment with soft-soap, or sauer-kraut. (D 61–63)

Like the gossipy introduction and the paddling adventure quoted earlier, this excerpt might stump some readers who think they know Poe's writing when they see it. Did Poe really care this much about street paving? About "pleasantness to the hoof"? Perhaps he did—he spent a lot of time walking the city streets, so it is not surprising that, almost a year later, in the *Broadway Journal*, he would again hold forth on the subject, not merely reprinting the long paragraph quoted above but expanding his claims on behalf of chemically treated wooden pavement. As Poe's most extensive writing about his experience in the city, "Doings of Gotham" defies our expectations of a "Poe-esque" style, at least partly because he was experimenting in a form that was new to him. Not surprisingly, the Willis-inspired tone of the first letter quickly gave way to the voice of a stodgy and somewhat cranky Knickerbocker, exasperated by Brooklyn architecture and bad pavement.

Sometime in May or early June, as Poe was writing the "Doings of Gotham" letters, he moved with Virginia and Maria to a farm owned by Patrick and Mary Brennan, a 216-acre parcel off Bloomingdale Road (now Broadway) near present-day Amsterdam Avenue and Eighty-Fourth Street. This relocation made sense to the Poe-Clemm trio: it would be healthier for Virginia to live away from the city, and the Brennans almost certainly offered more space at a lower cost than Poe could have secured in Lower Manhattan.[18] Though they stayed at the Brennan farm less than a year (probably seven or eight months), it was Poe's longest residence in Manhattan. We know relatively little about Poe's life with the Brennans, but the available evidence presents an intriguing scenario: during a pivotal period in his

Figure 4.3 Archival photograph, from about 1890, of the house at Brennan Farm, blended with a photograph of the approximate location at West Eighty-Fourth Street and Broadway. (Archival photograph of Brennan Farm House, Eighty-Fourth and Broadway, 1879, #84696d, courtesy of the New York Historical Society.)

Figure 4.4 Approximate location of "Brennan Farm," where Poe completed "The Raven" in 1844.

career, Poe chose to live about five miles north of what constituted the city and about six miles from the hub of periodical publishing. Poe was *in* New York and yet *outside of* New York, remote and secluded at a time when he was clearly not trying to remove himself from the publishing world. Throughout his residence with the Brennans, he wrote steadily—prodigiously, in fact—while planning the next step in his career.

According to Mrs. Brennan, Poe loved life in the country; as she told the early Poe biographer William F. Gill, "When not at his favorite seat by the river's brink, he would place himself at one of the front windows, and with Virginia by his side, watch for hours the fading glories of the summer evening skies." From his writing table, "[Poe] could look down upon the rolling waters of the Hudson and over at the Palisades beyond. It was a fitting dwelling for a poet, and though not far from the city's busy hum, the atmosphere of solitude and remoteness was as actual, as if the spot had been in the heart of the Rocky Mountains."[19] The Brennans' son-in-law, who never met Poe but recalled his mother-in-law's somewhat romanticized stories about him, added details for a newspaper story published in 1900: "It was Poe's custom to wander away from the house in pleasant weather to 'Mount Tom,' an immense rock, which may still be seen in Riverside Park, where he would sit alone for hours, gazing out upon the Hudson. Other days he would roam through the surrounding woods and, returning in the afternoon, sit in the 'big room,' as it used to be called, by a window and work unceasingly with pen and paper, until the evening shadows."[20]

Poe had moved to New York to advance his publishing career, and yet here he was living on a farm, physically detached from the swarm of magazine and newspaper offices in the city. He could have traveled downtown by omnibus, essentially a horse-drawn streetcar; in fact, he wrote a satiric article about omnibus travel for a Philadelphia newspaper that summer ("A wet umbrella and a dirty dog are useful in a full omnibus. When you enter and leave, tread upon the company's toes" [T 2:1091]).[21] But he probably walked more often than he rode, since walking was free and omnibus transport, only a little faster, required a fare.[22] Around October, Poe began working for N. P. Willis and George Pope Morris's *Evening Mirror* at 105 Nassau Street, which likely increased the frequency of these treks. Google Maps estimates what would have been Poe's walk at an hour and fifty-four minutes today; it probably took less time before the advent of automobiles and traffic lights, but, still, it is hard to imagine Poe covering that much ground in less than eighty or ninety minutes. By contrast, the Spring Garden home where the Poe family had lived in Philadelphia for the year prior to their removal to New York was semirural but still only about a twenty-minute walk to that city's center of publishing.

By the 1840s, American men with careers based in northeastern cities were beginning to embrace suburban living— "country life within city reach," as Willis himself represented it.[23] But the genteel lifestyle epitomized by Washington Irving's celebrated "Sunnyside" estate and Willis's "Idlewild" presumed an income that could sustain home ownership and the cost of commuting by steamboat, rail, or carriage. Poe may have aspired to this suburban ideal, but in 1844 he lived a poor man's version of it. Moreover, Poe's letters from Brennan Farm strongly suggest that he saw himself as isolated, not within comfortable reach of the city. On July 10 he told his correspondent Thomas Holly Chivers, "You will find me here—at New-York—where I live, [at] present, in strict seclusion, busied with books and [ambiti] ous thoughts" (L 1:453). Writing to his friend Frederick W.

Figure 4.5 An 1844 map of New York City, with developed areas shaded. Brennan Farm, where Poe, Maria, and Virginia lived throughout the second half of 1844, is literally off the map, well beyond the developed portion of the grid. The locations of Poe's three known residences in 1845 to early 1846 are marked. ("Plan von New-York, 1844," Lionel Pincus and Princess Firyal Map Division, New York Public Library Library Digital Collections.)

Thomas in September, he explained: "I have left Philadelphia, and am living, at present, about five miles out of New York. For the last seven or eight months I have been playing hermit in earnest—nor have I seen a living soul out of my family" (L 1:457). Finally, toward the end of his time with the Brennans, in early January 1845, he explained again to Thomas: "I do not live in town—very seldom visit it—and, of course, am not in the way of matters and things as I used to be. . . . In about three weeks, I shall move into the City, and recommence a life of activity under better auspices, I hope, than ever before. *Then* I may be able to do something" (L 1:475).[24] The slight inconsistencies in these references to his location are intriguing. To Chivers he is *at* New York but in strict intellectual seclusion, as if it is the mode of life he has chosen for himself. To Thomas he is *outside* New York. In the September letter he exaggerates the length of his hermitage, while in January he probably exaggerates in saying that he "seldom" visits the city. In fact, since he was now writing editorial filler for the *Evening Mirror*, he must have made frequent treks downtown. Furthermore, what seems like a deliberate choice in July comes across as an obstacle or as frustration in January. The limited available evidence suggests that Poe enjoyed and benefited from "playing hermit" even though he was increasingly frustrated by his physical separation from the hub of his profession.

When Poe referred to "better auspices," he was probably thinking of his delayed magazine project, the other consistent theme of his letters from Brennan Farm. In his letter to Chivers, he described himself as "busied with books and ambitious thoughts, until the hour shall arrive when I may come forth with a certainty of success. A Magazine like Graham's will never do. We must do something far better" (L 1:453). When he asked his friend Charles Anthon to help convince Harper & Brothers to publish a collection of his tales, he explained book publication was merely a means to that end; it would place him in "a far more advantageous position . . . in regard to the establishment of a Magazine" (L 1:471).

While still dreaming of his own magazine, Poe kept busy writing. In addition to "Doings of Gotham"—which he discontinued at the end of June—and his work for the *Evening Mirror*, he wrote, for various periodicals, satirical essays (one on urban transportation, another on cats), an article to accompany an engraved illustration of Byron and his niece Mary Ann Chaworth, and the first installments of a series for the *Democratic Review* called "Marginalia." This last was both column-filler and another experiment in journalistic personae, as Poe adopted the pose of a distinguished man of letters whose marginal annotations, presumably gleaned from a vast personal library, are rich with wit and insight—an idealized version of the rural literary "hermit" role he was playing in real life.

He also continued to publish a variety of fiction throughout 1844 and early 1845. In the second half of 1844, he published seven stories, written either just before or just after moving to New York: the spooky half-essay/half-tale "The Premature Burial"; the gothic love story "The Oblong Box"; "Mesmeric Revelation," a hoax that gave serious consideration to postmortem consciousness; a comic detective story, "Thou Art the Man!"; two broad comic spoofs, "The Angel of the Odd" and "The Literary Life of Thingum Bob, Esq."; and his intricate third and final story featuring the detective C. Auguste Dupin, "The Purloined Letter."[25] Another tale from this period, "The System of Doctor Tarr and Professor Fether," revolves around inmates taking control of an asylum. It might have been inspired partly by his previous residence near Eastern State Penitentiary, though, at

Brennan Farm, between the supposed completion of the manuscript and its publication, Poe was only a short walk from the Bloomingdale Insane Asylum, located near present-day Columbia University. Two more satirical stories, "Some Words with a Mummy" and "The Thousand-and-Second Tale of Scheherezade," were written at Brennan Farm and published in early 1845. This flurry of activity, both writing and seeing his work into print, solidifies the impression that Poe was in fact very busy—and, according to the Brennans, sober—throughout his semiseclusion, and that he was building a resume in New York with an eye to starting his own magazine. Dupin's characterization of his rival, the Minister D——, in "The Purloined Letter" might apply to Poe himself at Brennan Farm: "Perhaps, the most really energetic human being now alive—but that is only when nobody sees him" (T 2:990).

And yet two items written by Poe around this time reveal his cynicism toward the enterprise through which he hoped to achieve lasting renown. His bitter editorial on the need for international copyright, "Some Secrets of the Magazine Prison-House," offers a simple explanation for the popularity of the medium and the poor pay for authors: American firms would not publish American books when they could pirate popular British titles. Even so,

> it would *not do* (perhaps this is the idea) to let our poor devil authors absolutely starve, while we grow fat, in a literary sense, on the good things of which we unblushingly pick the pocket of all Europe: it would not be exactly the thing *comme il faut*, to permit a positive atrocity of this kind: and hence we have Magazines, and hence we have a portion of the public who subscribe to these Magazines (through sheer pity), and hence we have Magazine publishers (who sometimes take upon themselves the duplicate title of "editor *and*

proprietor,")—publishers, we say, who, under certain conditions of good conduct, occasional puffs, and decent subserviency at all times, make it a point of conscience to encourage the poor devil author with a dollar or two, more or less as he behaves himself properly and abstains from the indecent habit of turning up his nose. (T 2:1207)

Poe then proceeds to tell the story of one "poor devil author" who starves to death while waiting for payment from a magazine owner, who buys a meal of canvasback duck and champagne with the money saved. In the more jocular "Literary Life of Thingum Bob, Esq.," the fictional memoirist is a no-talent hack whose signature poem is a two-line ode to hair tonic. Thingum Bob claims to have risen to the top of the magazine world through "diligence," though his narrative reveals that his ability to navigate the shifting politics of literary coteries is his only marketable skill—and yet it is all he needs. Clearly, Poe still identified with the poor devil authors who struggled to survive while the Thingum Bobs of the world became rich and famous. And yet Poe may have believed that he was about to join the ranks of the editor-proprietors and one-trick poets he liked to ridicule.

Probably sometime during his last months in Philadelphia, Poe had written a draft of a narrative poem about a grief-stricken man visited by an ominous black bird. According to one former *Graham's* employee, he tried to sell the poem to his former boss, who rejected it but took up a small charitable collection for him.[26] After moving to New York, Poe revised and may have expanded the poem at Brennan Farm, then sold it to the *American Review*, a recently launched New York magazine. Part of the considerable lore surrounding the poem concerns the trifling payment Poe received from the *Review*: probably between nine and fifteen dollars.[27] However, there is no record of Poe complaining that he was inadequately compensated in this case; clearly more interested in the poem's circulation than in direct remuneration, he arranged with his boss N. P. Willis to publish it in the *Evening Mirror* days in advance of its appearance in the *Review*. Willis not only printed the poem but introduced it as being "unsurpassed in English poetry for subtle conception, masterly ingenuity of versification, and consistent, sustaining of imaginative lift and 'pokerishness' [that is, spookiness]. . . . It will stick to the memory of everybody who reads it" (P 361). He was right: "The Raven" was an instant sensation, and Poe would be closely identified with the poem not only for the rest of his career, but for all time.

Mrs. Brennan and her son-in-law promoted the idea that, while working on "The Raven," Poe gained inspiration from the farmhouse's upstairs chamber, where he worked. According to General O'Beirne, a bust of Pallas sat on a shelf above the door, and the Brennans' daughter Martha, O'Beirne's future wife, arranged the manuscript pages that Poe tossed to the floor as he revised.[28] I want to avoid both the convenient conclusion that country air and hospitality gave Poe the peace of mind to transform the early version that Graham rejected into his masterpiece, and a simple identification of Poe, writing "The Raven" in the Brennans' upstairs room, as the poem's speaker in his chamber surrounded by forgotten lore. And yet . . . Poe clearly felt isolated from the everyday life of his profession, even as he was writing and publishing at a brisk pace. "The Raven" features an excess of "inner" activity—the speaker's grief-inspired fantasies about the meaning of the bird's appearance and repeated utterance—within the virtual absence of "outer" or physical action, especially remarkable for a popular narrative poem. It is not only about loss but also about seclusion, setting up an invasion of privacy that is simultaneously dreaded and welcome.

While it dramatizes a private episode, "The Raven" was designed for public consumption: to be read aloud, on a stage, as Poe himself did many times. Indeed, there is little doubt that Poe knew he had written a blockbuster. Before its publication, he shared the poem with his friend and fellow poet William Ross Wallace, declaring it "the greatest poem that was ever written."[29] Poe later told his friend F. W. Thomas that he "wrote it for the express purpose of running," that is, being widely circulated (L 1:505). The poem "ran" quickly through New York and throughout the country, with parodies appearing almost immediately. The poet Elizabeth Oakes Smith recalled that in early 1845 "the Raven became known everywhere, and everyone was saying 'Nevermore.'"[30] Like the volume of tales he hoped Anthon would convince the Harpers to publish, "The Raven" was likely, in Poe's calculation, a means to his ultimate end: the high-quality magazine that he would control, and that would make him financially independent. In this sense "The Raven" does mirror Poe's working life at Brennan Farm in its productive tension between the psychic comfort of privacy and the need to go public; the poem is a showy tour de force about interior experience.

About a week before the publication of "The Raven," Poe enjoyed a publicity bump in the form of a biographical article by James Russell Lowell, prominently placed in *Graham's Magazine*. Lowell, who was friendly with Poe at the time, told him that he wrote the article "to please you rather than the public," and Poe certainly must have been pleased. Lowell described Poe's "genius" as a combination of "vigorous yet minute analysis" and "a wonderful fecundity of imagination." He acknowledged Poe's critical severity—a trait Poe actually prided himself on—and suggested that the remedy for the overly caustic reviews would be for Poe to control his own magazine. The one-two punch of Lowell's

article and "The Raven" seem coordinated, especially con-
sidering that Poe's friend and employer Willis advertised
both, conspicuously republishing the biography in the *Evening Mirror* and adding, "We wonder, by the way, that,
with so fine a critic at command for an editor, some New
York publisher does not establish a Monthly Review, de-
voted exclusively to high critical purposes."[31]

In short, Poe was making his move toward fulfilling his
magazine dream in early 1845, which required making another kind of move, leaving the Brennan Farm for a residence in Lower Manhattan—specifically, 154 Greenwich
Street, on the eastern edge of what is now the World Trade
Center complex. Like all of New York in the 1840s, this
neighborhood between Broadway and the Hudson River
was in transition; as the area became increasingly commercial, the residences that remained were cheaper and less desirable than those to the north, near and above Washington
Square.[32] But it was a convenient location: Poe now lived
within ten minutes' walking distance of virtually every publishing office in the city. He was also living close to New
York's more affluent literati, and, after the publication of
"The Raven," they were eager to make his acquaintance.
The writer Henry Tuckerman described Poe's visit in early
1845 to a gathering at the home of physician and socialite
John W. Francis, where he was known only by reputation:

> The expression on [Francis's] face, as he left the room beto-
> kened the visit of a celebrity; in a few moments he ushered
> into the room a pale, thin, and most grave-looking man,
> whose dark dress and solemn air, with the Doctor's own
> look of ceremonious gravity, produced an ominous silence,
> where a moment before, all was hilarity; slowly conducting
> his guest around the table, and turning to his wife, he waved
> his hand, and, with elaborate courtesy, made this unique

announcement: "The Raven!" and certainly no human physiognomy more resembled that bird than the stranger's, who, without a smile or a word, bowed slightly and slowly.[33]

Similarly, at the Greenwich Village home of the popular author and editor Caroline Kirkland, "there was great curiosity to see the writer of that wonderful poem," according to another witness.[34] Poe began attending literary salons hosted by the poet and socialite Anne Charlotte Lynch, where established New York writers of both sexes mingled and recited poetry. These genteel, nonalcoholic events encouraged Poe's best behavior and, for a while, enhanced his reputation.

He was also courted by "Young America," a New York–based movement promoting literary and cultural nationalism, spearheaded by the *Democratic Review* and its editor, John O' Sullivan (best known for coining the phrase "manifest destiny"). It was an unlikely alliance: although he never committed himself to partisan politics, Poe was particularly no Democrat, as he distrusted what he would call "mobocracy" associated with the party of Andrew Jackson. While in Philadelphia, he had sought a government job through connections with the son of president John Tyler, a Whig. As for literary nationalism, Poe had consistently opposed promoting novels and poems on the basis of their American content or patriotic themes, and yet he did share common ground with Young America on the need for international copyright, which would supposedly encourage the publication of more American-authored works.[35] During his brief association with the group, Poe editorialized on behalf of the copyright cause; in return, their pundits promoted him. Not coincidentally, Poe's first book publications in five years—*Tales* and *The Raven and Other Poems*—were included in Wiley and Putnam's patriotically titled Library of

American Books series, edited by another leader of the Young America movement, Evert Duyckinck.

As another sign of Poe's new renown, on February 28, 1845, an audience of about three hundred turned out to hear him lecture on "The Poets and Poetry of America" at the Society Library, Leonard Street and Broadway. Duyckinck, among others, promoted the event: "What mode of discussion Mr. Poe will adopt, we cannot pretend to say; but the lecture will differ from anything he has ever done before, if it do[es] not prove novel, ingenious, and a capital antidote to dullness."[36] The lecture was a turning point for Poe's fortunes in New York, yet it exemplified his career-long tendency to sow calamity from the ground of success. At this moment Poe was as well known and well regarded as he would ever be in his lifetime, lecturing at a prestigious venue with a hit poem ringing in everyone's ear. The lecture was covered by numerous local magazines and newspapers, with mostly favorable assessments, particularly from writers already in his corner. And yet, building on his reputation as an exacting critic, Poe, somewhat predictably, dispensed more censure than praise, singling out a number of celebrated poets for criticism and suggesting that one of them, the beloved Henry Wadsworth Longfellow, borrowed excessively from other poets. Poe had made a similar claim against Longfellow in *Burton's* in 1840, but now he seemed intent on a full-scale campaign. In a recent review in the *Mirror* he had insinuated, with no real evidence, that Longfellow was a plagiarist, and he doubled down on the claim at the Society Library. Whether Poe was just following his own instincts and literary principles, or he truly believed that there was no such thing as bad publicity, he was overstepping: a potentially libelous campaign against Longfellow was not the way to endear himself to the very people who could help sustain his current popularity and realize his long-delayed monthly magazine. Even though Poe had made his pre-"Raven" reputation as a "Tomahawk Man," and even though he could play the scrappy Gothamite to Longfellow's privileged Brahmin Harvard professor, he should have known that his one-sided "Longfellow War" would damage only his, not Longfellow's, reputation.

The day after Poe's lecture, the *Evening Mirror* published a long letter—signed "Outis" (Greek for "nobody")—refuting Poe's charge against Longfellow and insinuating that Poe himself was a plagiarist. Scholars disagree over whether Poe wrote the "Outis" letter himself, but even if he didn't create his own sparring partner, he enjoyed having one. He responded to Outis with a lengthy article in the *Broadway Journal*, a new weekly paper, and continued his disquisition on Longfellow and the nature of plagiarism over the next four issues, with an addendum in Thomas Dunn English's magazine the *Aristidean*. Poe's relentless war with Longfellow created yet another sensation, but his charges were virtually groundless; Longfellow, taking the high road, never responded in print.[37] Mutual friends of the two authors were puzzled: George Rex Graham wrote to Longfellow, asking, "What has 'broke loose' in Poe?" and James Russell Lowell similarly distanced himself from the writer he had recently lauded.[38] Meanwhile, Boston papers began publicly mocking the famous author of "The Raven."[39]

Around the same time that Graham was wondering what had broken loose in Poe, his former employee sent him an article—half essay, half fiction—that might have offered a clue. "The Imp of the Perverse" develops an idea Poe had hinted at in "The Black Cat" a few years earlier: that human beings commonly experience a "perverse" or irrational desire to do what we know we should not. As Poe describes it, the "Imp of the Perverse" is not so much an urge to violate the law or a moral code as an urge to subvert our own designs, a self-destructive tendency. After several pages of discursive, quasi-philosophical commentary on his theory, the article shifts to a condensed narrative similar to "The Tell-Tale Heart" and "The Black Cat." The erudite philosopher we have been listening to (and assuming to be the author) has himself committed the perfect crime, having killed his victim with a poisoned candle. Days later, while inwardly congratulating himself, he encounters his own "imp": he thinks to himself, "I am safe—I am safe," but then adds, "Yes—if I be not fool enough to make open confession!" (T 1225) With that thought, his fate is sealed, as he cannot control his own impulse to confess and ensure his own execution. By analogy, at the moment Poe achieved the kind of success that should have given him control of his own magazine and his own career, he began undermining that very success, as if listening to his own imp.

As Poe carried out his Longfellow campaign, he was also becoming more involved with a new weekly paper, the *Broadway Journal*. Launched in January 1845 by the popular fiction writer C. F. Briggs and publisher John Bisco, the sixteen-page *Journal* covered literature and other arts, primarily (though not exclusively) focused on New York. Briggs chose the name, he said, "because it is indigenous, and furthermore is indicative of the spirit which we intend shall characterize our paper. Broadway is confessedly the finest street in the first city of the New World. It is the great artery through which flows the best blood of our system."[40] The *Broadway Journal* was housed near City Hall, a block north of the *Mirror*'s offices and about half a mile from Poe's Greenwich Street residence. Briggs was greatly impressed with Poe, who began contributing reviews with the first issue; in March he made Poe a coeditor, along with Briggs himself and art critic Henry C. Watson. But by the summer Briggs, Poe, and Bisco were already embroiled in a power struggle. Poe had not worn well on Briggs, who complained of his drinking and general selfishness. But it was Briggs who was either pushed out or left, and in October Poe suddenly became sole editor and co-owner with Bisco, then bought out Bisco with borrowed money. Somewhat unexpectedly, Poe had finally gained control of his own periodical, but the weekly paper, though respectable, fell short, and was now falling even shorter, of the high-quality literary monthly he had been planning for years. More urgently, it was losing money, which is probably why Poe's partners were willing to leave it in his hands. As sole "editor and proprietor," Poe was unable to save the *Journal*; after a brief partnership with another investor and desperate efforts to sustain the operation—twelve- to fourteen-hour workdays, borrowing money from anyone who would lend—Poe folded the paper one year after its inception, three months after taking it over.

Though Poe had worked hard in the final months to keep it afloat, the *Journal*'s demise had been hastened by his inability to stay sober after moving back downtown. As had been the case in Philadelphia, drinking damaged his reputation: in April, the *Town*, another New York weekly, included in a satirical list of forthcoming books "A treatise on 'Aqua Pura,' its uses and abuses, by Edgar A. Poe . . . to be issued at the Broadway Journal office."[41] Briggs complained repeatedly about Poe's drinking, and Lowell, meeting Poe in person for the first time in May 1845, found him "a little tipsy, as if he were recovering from a fit of drunkenness, & with that over-solemnity with which men in such cases try to convince you of their sobriety."[42] Visiting from Georgia, the poet Thomas Holley Chivers met Poe for the first time that summer and found him by turns either drunk or recovering from a bout of drunkenness.[43] By the time of Chivers's visit, the family had moved again, this time about a mile and a half west to 195 East Broadway on the Lower East Side—less central than lower Greenwich Street, but probably cheaper and also quieter. Within a few months, though, Poe would move yet again, settling in Greenwich Village at 85 Amity (now West Third) Street, just south of Washington Square—a building that remained standing until 2002, when it was razed by New York University. Poe might have left the East Broadway house because of a dispute over rent, or inability to pay; he later wrote that "I did not leave it on very good terms with the landlady" (L 1:591). The family's new lodgings were small and modest, but they were in a more respectable neighborhood. In fact, Anne C. Lynch, who hosted the literary salons Poe attended throughout 1845, lived just a few blocks away on Waverly Place.[44]

The frequent moves underscore Poe's general instability following the sudden success of "The Raven," and he was never more unstable than when he was away from home altogether. In October, having been invited—through Lowell's efforts—to present a new poem at the Boston Lyceum, Poe ignited another war of words. Finding himself unable to compose a new work, Poe read his long poetic fantasy "Al Aaraaf," first published in 1829 and temporarily renamed "The Messenger Star." Accounts of his performance that evening vary, but he seems to have acquitted himself reasonably well and could have gone back to New York relieved either that no one noticed he was recycling an old poem or that no one cared. Instead, upon his return, Poe began boasting in the *Journal* of having "quizzed" (conned) the Bostonians by delivering an incomprehensible "juvenile poem," and claiming that the undiscriminating Lyceum audience loved it. As he had done during the Longfellow War, he used the *Broadway Journal* as a platform to spar with the Boston literary establishment, this time represented by Cornelia Wells Walter, editor of the *Evening Transcript*. At one point Poe made the self-contradictory jab, "We like

Boston. We were born there——and perhaps it is just as well not to mention that we are heartily ashamed of the fact" (E 1086). For her part, Walter dished out disparaging puns on Poe's last name and took at least one dig at his reputation for drunkenness. When he solicited "support" for the *Journal* from its "friends," she quipped sarcastically, "What a question to ask! Edgar A. Poe to be in a condition to require *support*! It is indeed remarkable."[45]

Meanwhile, Poe was no longer endearing himself to the New York literary circle that had embraced him upon the success of "The Raven." Chivers recalled Poe staying home, pretending to be sick, to avoid having to deliver a poem to "one of the Literary Societies of the City."[46] More seriously, in early 1846 Poe found himself at the center of scandal involving his relationships with women writers he had encountered through the literary salons. In March 1845, he met Frances Sargent Locke Osgood, a popular poet married to a society portrait painter. Attracted to each other, Poe and Osgood wrote—and published—flirtatious poems, whose intended recipients would have been obvious to any discerning reader as well their own circle. For instance, the *Broadway Journal*, with Poe's name on the masthead, published a poem by Osgood that alludes to Poe's poems "Israfel" and "The Raven," describing a secret love:

I know a noble heart that beats

For one it loves how "wildly well!"
I only know for *whom* it beats;
But I must never tell!

Never tell!
Hush! Hark! How Echo soft repeats,—
Ah! *Never* tell![47]

In early 1846, another salon habitué, Elizabeth Ellet, visited Poe's house in Greenwich Village and saw what she considered a compromising letter from Osgood to Poe. Osgood later claimed that she had nothing to hide; moreover, she was friendly with Virginia Poe, and was known to visit the Poes at their home on Amity Street.[48] Yet, at Ellet's urging, Osgood sent a pair of emissaries, journalist Margaret Fuller and poet Anne C. Lynch, to retrieve her letters. Poe was taken aback by this visit and retorted that Ellet should be more concerned about retrieving her *own* letters to him, a remark that escalated the squabble. By the time this soap opera had run its course, Poe had gotten into a fistfight with his sometime friend Thomas Dunn English, after English refused to lend him a pistol to defend himself from Ellet's outraged brother. Poe managed to escape the scandal without further violence, but he and English, whose relationship was already on shaky ground, became bitter enemies.

Poe had hoped that the publicity from Lowell's biographical profile and, even more, the success of "The Raven" would lead, finally, to his establishing a high-quality monthly magazine, and the literary stature that came with it. Whether he moved downtown specifically to be near the *Broadway Journal* office or just to be in close contact with the publishing world, he was there in pursuit of that goal. Sadly, Poe's plan fell just short: the *Journal* was not the *Stylus*, his literary battles with New England did not make him a champion of the New York literati, and personal networking opportunities eventually fell prey to bouts of drinking and scandal. After a highly productive 1844, Poe wrote little fiction or poetry in 1845, occupied as he was with book and theater reviews, the Longfellow War, and other editorial work for the *Journal*. In this year in which he had achieved his greatest fame, he earned only about seven hundred dollars (roughly equivalent to twenty thousand dollars today).[49] With the *Journal*'s collapse, an exhausted Poe must have seen that it was time for another removal from the city.

For Valentine's Day, 1846, Virginia wrote a poem for Edgar, an acrostic spelling out his name with the first letter of each line, expressing not only her love but also her wish for the future:

Ever with thee I wish to roam—
Dearest my life is thine.
Give me a cottage for my home
And a rich old cypress vine,
Removed from the world with its sin and care
And the tattling of many tongues.
Love alone shall guide us when we are there—
Love shall heal my weakened lungs;
And Oh, the tranquil hours we'll spend,
Never wishing that others may see!
Perfect ease we'll enjoy, without thinking to lend
Ourselves to the world and its glee—
Ever peaceful and blissful we'll be.[50]

As they had done two years earlier, the family moved north of the developed portion of Manhattan, this time to Turtle Bay, near the East River. Poe, Virginia, and Maria might have lived briefly with the Brennans again before boarding with the Miller family, whose riverfront property was located on what is now part of the United Nations headquarters, near Forty-Seventh Street. The Millers' son and daughter—nine and twelve years old at the time, respectively—both provided fond reminiscences many years later, the only record of Poe's having lived there. The daughter described them as near neighbors who would "frequently call on us," Poe sometimes borrowing a boat so that he could row out to the islands south of Blackwell's to swim. The son claimed that Poe actually lived *with* the Miller family, having "prevailed upon my parents to accommodate him until he could find a place where they could keep house for themselves."[51]

The place the Poe family eventually found, in May or thereabout, was much farther north, in Fordham: part of the new township of West Farms, in what would become known later in the nineteenth century as the Bronx. For less than nine dollars a month, Poe rented a small cottage on a triangular acre of land, about ten minutes' walk from a recently established stop on the New York and Harlem railroad line. The area was lightly populated, but thanks to the railroad it was beginning to attract development, including the houses of some wealthy families.[52] It was, by all accounts, bucolic: the property on which the cottage sat was bounded on one side by an apple orchard, there were other fruit trees in the yard, and the nearest neighbor was the recently founded St. John's College (which became Fordham University in the twentieth century). One visitor, J. H. Hopkins, later recalled Poe complimenting the Jesuit priests of St. John's as "highly cultivated gentlemen and scholars" who "smoked, drank, and played cards like gentlemen, and never said a word about religion."[53] The cottage, which was about thirty years old, was small and sparsely furnished, but tidy, thanks to Muddy Clemm's diligence. Trains arrived at and departed from Fordham six times daily, with service to city hall, near the center of publishing. Poe could have commuted regularly, but at this point he had no place of employment, little money for train fare, and apparently little inclination to make frequent trips to the city, preferring to send Muddy to solicit or deliver manuscripts, or to collect payment. He claimed to be, and probably was, ill much of the time, and he was also preoccupied with Virginia's worsening condition.

But, even from Fordham, Poe continued to stir controversy, most conspicuously with a new series for *Godey's Lady's Book* called "The Literati of New York City." Published in Philadelphia, *Godey's* was the highest-circulation

Figure 4.6 Poe's cottage in Poe Park, the Bronx. In 1913, the house was moved a short distance from its original location in order to preserve it.

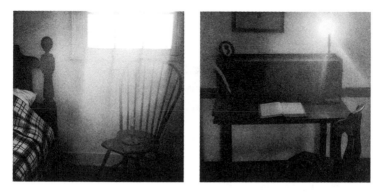

Figure 4.7 The interior of the Bronx Poe Cottage as it appears today.

monthly magazine in the United States, so Poe had a big national stage for his pronouncements on local literary personalities. "The Literati" was an immediate sensation—not for the admiring sketches Poe offered of authors such as the Reverend George Bush or Caroline Kirkland, but for his score-settling takedowns, particularly of his former *Broadway Journal* partner C. F. Briggs in the first installment and former friend Thomas Dunn English in the second. After accusing English of plagiarizing poetry, Poe dismissed his ability as a magazine editor: "No spectacle can be more pitiable than that of a man without the commonest school education busying himself in attempts to instruct mankind on topics of polite literature" (E 1166–67). As a final, gratuitous taunt, Poe pretended not to know English personally, despite their long history. The first installment sparked a run on the May 1846 *Godey's*; *New-York Tribune* editor Horace Greeley told a friend that "every copy is bought up in the City. I have applied twice without success."[54] Advertising the June issue, publisher Louis A. Godey promised to reprint the first "Literati" along with the second because "we have had orders for hundreds from Boston and New York which we could not supply."[55] In June, English struck back hard in the pages of the *Evening/Weekly Mirror*, which was no longer under N. P. Willis's Poe-friendly editorial control. In addition to resurrecting the Osgood-Ellet affair and Poe's embarrassing attempt to borrow a gun for self-defense, English characterized his antagonist as a drunkard, "unprincipled, base, and depraved," and accused him of having committed forgery and having obtained money (from English himself) under false pretenses. After another published exchange, Poe filed suit against the *Mirror*'s owners for libel.

With the October issue of *Godey's*, the "Literati" series had run its course, but the controversy hadn't. Throughout

1846 rumors had already been spreading, in print, that Poe was mentally ill. English depicted him as crazed as well as drunk through a thinly veiled caricature—a character named Marmaduke Hammerhead, known for his poem "Black Crow"—in his novel *1844, or the Power of the S. F.*, serialized in the *Mirror*. Word got out regarding the Poe family's current state of poverty, which led to some sympathetic, but also sanctimonious, editorial comments in the New York papers.

In the same issue of *Godey's* that concluded the "Literati" series, Poe published his most enduring story from this period, "The Cask of Amontillado." Appropriately, it is a fantasy of revenge, in which a fallen member of an aristocratic social circle entombs his more prosperous rival—the not-so-subtly named Fortunato—by outsmarting him, using reverse psychology and manipulating his victim's pride in his own expertise in wine. Feigning concern for Fortunato's health, the less fortunate Montresor tells him, "You are rich, respected, admired, beloved; you are happy, as I once was. You are a man to be missed. For me it is no matter" (T 2:1259). While this brilliant tale can't be reduced to a fictionalized rendering of Poe's relationship with English or any other member of the New York literati, Montresor's thirst for revenge, his proclaimed motivation of honor barely concealing his jealousy, resonate with Poe's literary battles. Yet some part of Poe may be glimpsed not only in the ingenious killer but also in the victim, whose undoing is a drunken quest for another bottle of wine.

The demise of the *Broadway Journal*, the Longfellow War, the Osgood-Ellet scandal, the infamy of the "Literati" series: Poe was careening from one controversy to the next while trying to maintain a peaceful home life in Fordham. But, despite its pastoral setting, the Fordham cottage was hardly an escape, as Virginia lay dying throughout Poe's professional misadventures. Finally, on January 30, 1847, five years after her symptoms first became apparent, Virginia's suffering ended. Edgar, distraught, remained in near-seclusion in Fordham for the rest of the year, except for a midsummer trip to Washington and Philadelphia. He received expressions of sympathy and assistance from friends and admirers, but in his grief he became even more estranged from the city's literary scene. Enlisted that fall by an elocution instructor to write "something suitable for recitation embodying thoughts that would admit of vocal variety and expression" (P 410), Poe delivered "Ulalume," a poem as sonically hypnotic as "The Raven," treading the same thematic territory. But the two poems make for very different reading experiences: while "The Raven," immediately accessible, nearly gallops as its speaker's anguish builds to a near frenzy, the repetition and alliteration in "Ulalume" create a slow, viscous movement:

> The skies they were ashen and sober;
>
>> The leaves they were crispéd and sere—
>> The leaves they were withering and sere:
>> It was night, in the lonesome October
>>> Of my most immemorial year:
>> It was hard by the dim lake of Auber,
>>> In the misty mid region of Weir:—
>> It was down by the dank tarn of Auber,
>>> In the ghoul-haunted woodland of Weir. (P 415–16)

The speaker, joined by "Psyche, my soul," is guided by "Astarte's bediamonded crescent"—either the planet Venus or some star of love. In this dreamscape, the speaker repeatedly suggests that there is something portentous about this "night of the year," and Psyche warns him not to follow Astarte's light, but, by the poem's end, he finds himself at the grave of his lost love Ulalume on the anniversary of her burial. Of course, the speaker should have known where he was going, but his journey ends in anguish, the verbal repetition now fraught with sorrowful meaning:

Well I know, now, this dim lake of Auber—

This misty mid region of Weir:—
Well I know, now, this dank tarn of Auber—
This ghoul-haunted woodland of Weir. (P 418)

Making the most of its elocutionary-lesson sound effects, the murky, dreamlike confusion of this poem of sorrow, written in the months after Virginia's death, viscerally conveys the sensation of grief, the inevitability of returning to that place of sorrow and loss.

Not long after Virginia's death, Poe was awarded $225 in his libel suit against the *Mirror*. He needed the money, but the ruling was hardly vindication in the eyes of the literary community, since Poe had, in a sense, trolled Thomas Dunn English, resorting to a lawsuit in the midst of a verbal battle *he* had instigated. Poe had all but given up writing fiction ("Cask" being the notable exception) and poetry (nothing significant since "The Raven" in early 1845), devoting most of his energy to the "Literati" series and reviews for *Godey's Lady's Book*. That trend away from fiction continued after Virginia's death, as he turned his attention to something completely different: his theory of the universe, a lecture and treatise that he would title *Eureka*. Poe posited that the universe originated in an event much like a big bang, and argued that, having expanded to its limit, gravity would pull everything back, and then the process would repeat: "A novel Universe swelling into existence, and then subsiding into nothingness, at every throb of the Heart Divine" (EU 103). Published in mid-1848 by G. P. Putnam, the 143-page cosmology did not sell well, but Poe still regarded it as his crowning achievement; a year after its publication, he would tell Maria, "I have no desire to live since I have done 'Eureka.' I could accomplish nothing more" (L 2:820).

Indeed, *Eureka* temporarily reenergized Poe: in a February 1848 letter to his friend George Eveleth in which he outlined the essay's argument, he also declared himself sober and in good health, acknowledging that his reputation might suggest otherwise:

> My *habits* are rigorously abstemious and I omit nothing of the natural regimen requisite for health:—i.e.—I rise early, eat moderately, drink nothing but water, and take abundant and regular exercise in the open air. But this is my private life—my studious and literary life—and of course escapes the eye of the world. The desire for society comes upon me only when I have become excited by drink. Then *only* I go—that is, at these times only I *have been* in the practice of going among my friends: who seldom, or in fact never, having seen me unless excited, take it for granted that I am always so. Those who *really* know me, know better. . . . But enough of this: the causes which maddened me to the drinking point are no more, and I am done drinking, forever. (L 2:648)

Poe might have overstated the division between his wholesome private life and his behavior while "among friends," but visitors to Fordham supported his claims of sobriety there. For air and exercise, he frequently walked along the High Bridge, which spanned the Harlem River as part of the Croton Aqueduct system that brought water to Manhattan.[56]

Four years after his optimistic letter describing the bountiful boardinghouse fare, Poe had come to see the city, correctly, as hazardous to his health, perhaps as much as it had been for Virginia's. The primary "cause" that he referred to

Figure. 4.8 The High Bridge, which spans the Harlem River, was completed during Poe's residence in the Bronx as part of the Croton Aqueduct system. It reopened for pedestrian and bicycle use in 2015.

in his letter to Eveleth was almost certainly Virginia's long, ultimately fatal illness; a year after her death, he could reasonably believe that he was making a healthy new start, but it's telling that he expressed no desire to return to Manhattan. Meanwhile, he renewed his efforts to establish the *Stylus* and began lecturing again, with a *Eureka*-based talk on "The Universe" at Society Library in February 1848. For the moment, Poe seemed stable and content in his retreat across the Harlem River. His past four years in New York had been among the most tumultuous of his life, as he moved in and out of the city while creating one sensation after another, trying to conquer the literary capital of the nation. As was so often the case, he had come tantalizingly close before his goal fell out of reach.

CHAPTER 5

In Transit (1848–1849)

Each of the previous chapters has focused on Poe's experience in a specific city, while chronicling a discreet period of his life. This last chapter has no such anchor. Although Poe still called Fordham home—it was, if nothing else, where his beloved mother-in-law could be found—he was away from the little cottage and from New York for almost half of the last fifteen months of his life and all of his last three. He spent the summer and fall of 1848 shuttling between Fordham, New York; Richmond, Virginia; Providence, Rhode Island; and Lowell, Massachusetts; then, after spending the first half of 1849 mostly in Fordham, he hit the road again, spending most of the summer in Richmond before his ill-fated attempt to return home.

In a sense, living out of a suitcase or a trunk was the story of Poe's life. Despite nearly four years spent at the "old place" near Rittenhouse Square in Philadelphia and the relative stability of Fordham, Poe changed addresses an average of once a year. After breaking with the Allans, he had found a family with Virginia and Maria Clemm, but he never put down roots in a community. As a young man, he had considered Richmond to be "home," but since leaving the *Southern Literary Messenger* in 1837 he had been merely an infrequent visitor there. His devotion to Muddy comes through in his letters throughout his travels, as well as his poem "To My Mother": "You who are more than mother unto me, / And fill my heart of hearts, where Death installed you / In setting my Virginia's spirit free" (P 467). And yet that bond of maternal affection was not enough for Poe to feel "at home" with her in Fordham. He wanted a wife, and he was bound to keep moving until he found one. His other motivation during this final, unsettled period was his career-long magazine ambition and the quest for subscribers. As he traveled from city to city, those two goals—marriage and a magazine—were constant.

During Virginia's illness, Poe had developed a close relationship with a Manhattan housewife named Marie Louise Shew, who had learned about the family's troubles through a friend and volunteered to nurse Virginia and provide comfort as well as material aid to Edgar. There is no suggestion of a romantic attachment in their correspondence, but clearly her feelings for Poe, and his for her, ran deep. The non-churchgoing Poe even accompanied "Loui" to a midnight service at the Episcopal Church of the Holy Communion at Sixth Avenue and Twentieth Street in late 1847. Their friendship continued after Virginia's death but ended as a consequence of Poe's publishing *Eureka* in June 1848. Shew's friend John Henry Hopkins Jr., a theology student, published reviews of both the lecture and print versions of Poe's cosmology, and even met with Poe to discuss his work. Hopkins initially admired much about the treatise but was scandalized by its author's overt pantheism, and he convinced the devout Mrs. Shew to cut her ties with Poe. She did, and Poe's written response to Shew has a familiar ring—a mixture of manipulation through guilt and sincere dejection—as well as a sadly accurate premonition: "Are you to vanish like all I love, or desire, from my darkened and 'lost soul' . . . unless some true and tender and pure womanly love saves me, I shall hardly last a year longer alone!" (L 2:677–78).

Meanwhile, other women were taking an interest in the newly widowed Poe, who was still in his thirties and well known, if not financially well off. Jane Ermina Locke, a poet from Lowell, began corresponding with him a few weeks after Virginia's death. She visited him in Fordham and invited him to Lowell around the same time his friendship with Loui Shew was dissolving in mid-1848. Meeting her in person, Poe learned what he had been unable to uncover through Locke's letters: that she was married with five children. Poe agreed to a lecture, arranged by Locke, in Lowell that July, but otherwise he tried to distance himself from her, partly because of her marital status, perhaps more because he didn't find her very appealing, but mostly because, during his visit to Lowell, he became infatuated with a woman Locke introduced him to—her neighbor Nancy Richmond.

Unfortunately for Poe, Richmond was also married, but, even though he had no intention of carrying on a sexual affair with her, he repeatedly expressed his devotion in letters throughout the next year. He would include a thinly fictionalized description of her in his story "Landor's Cottage," in which the narrator encounters "a young woman about twenty-eight years of age—slender, or rather slight, and somewhat above the medium height. . . . I said to myself, 'Surely here I have found the perfection of natural, in contradistinction from artificial *grace*.' . . . So intense an expression of romance, perhaps I should call it, or of unworldliness, as that which gleamed from her deep-set eyes, had never so sunk into my heart of hearts before" (T 2:1338–39). Poe named this idealized fictional creation "Annie," the same name he bestowed on Nancy Richmond not long after meeting her. For her part, Annie (who adopted the new name) regarded Poe as someone apart from, implicitly above, the ordinary run of men: "He seemed so *unlike* any other person, I had ever known, that I could not think of him in the same way—he was incomparable—not to be measured by any ordinary standard—& all the events of his life, which he narrated to me, had a flavor of *unreality* about them, just like his stories."[1]

Mrs. Richmond's husband Charles, a successful paper manufacturer, tolerated Poe's chaste adoration of his wife—at least initially—but, even so, Poe must have realized that the "true and tender and pure womanly love" that he needed to save him would not come from a married woman living two hundred miles from Fordham. So he hoped instead that it might come from Sarah Helen Whitman, who, much like Frances Osgood a few years earlier, established a relationship with Poe by publishing a love poem she wrote for him. Whitman, a widow living in Providence, was sufficiently connected to New York City salon culture to send a valentine—a poem titled "To Edgar A. Poe"—to one of Anne Lynch's literary gatherings in February 1848. Lynch, who was collecting the salon poems for publication, explained to Whitman that, while she admired her verses "exceedingly," she hesitated to publish a tribute to Poe, who by this point was "in such bad odour with most persons who visit me that if I were to receive him, I should lose the company of many whom I value more."[2] But Whitman, who would receive multiple warnings about Poe's reputation throughout their courtship, persisted, and Lynch helped her publish the poem—which addresses Poe as "the Raven," concluding, "Not a bird that roams the forest / Shall our lofty eyrie share"—in N. P. Willis's magazine the *Home Journal*. That got Poe's attention. He sent Helen a copy of his early poem "To Helen," cut from a copy of *The Raven and Other Poems*, then followed up with a new, 66-line blank-verse poem (posthumously titled "To Helen" as well).[3] In late September, Poe traveled to Providence to meet her.

Poe's travels in the second half of 1848 also included a visit to Richmond, the city where he had grown up, ostensibly to enlist subscribers and support for the *Stylus*. While he was there, he paid a surprise visit to the woman to whom he had been secretly engaged as a teenager: Elmira Royster, now the widowed Elmira Shelton. Poe was testing the waters for a renewed courtship, but Elmira was ambivalent about the attentions of an impoverished and somewhat notorious writer. She probably was not even aware that, while in Richmond, Poe tried to challenge a hostile editor, John M. Daniel, to a duel before cooler heads prevailed.[4] Lecturing, promoting the *Stylus*, pursuing a new wife and/or soul mate, Poe was spending little time in Fordham.

Travel for Poe, like most northeasterners, meant a combination of railroad and steamboat. Rail travel had gone from experimental to ubiquitous during Poe's adult life; by the year after his death, the United States would have some nine thousand miles of rail. Ralph Waldo Emerson observed that "Americans take to this contrivance, the railroad, as if it were the cradle in which they were born."[5] In 1854 Emerson's friend Henry David Thoreau, recognizing the tyrannical potential of new technology, warned, "We do not ride upon the railroad, it rides upon us," but even Thoreau also expressed a kind of admiration for the locomotive as a symbol of self-reliant determination. The actual experience of riding on a mid-nineteenth-century train was probably both exhilarating—moving at the unheard-of speed of twenty miles per hour—and nauseating. Dickens, in his *American Notes*, referred to the cars as "shabby omnibuses," and Fanny Kemble's description suggests the nineteenth-century equivalent of traveling on a small, no-frills commuter jet: "The windows . . . form the walls on each side of the carriage, which looks like a long greenhouse upon wheels; the seats, which each contain two persons (a pretty tight fit, too), are placed down the whole length of the vehicle, one behind the other, leaving a species of aisle in the middle for the uneasy (a large portion of the traveling community here) to fidget up and down, for the tobacco-chewers to spit in, and for a whole tribe of itinerant fruit and cake-sellers to rush through."[6]

Even as rail was revolutionizing travel, in the late 1840s there was nothing like a national rail *system*; short lines served local and regional customers, and they did not always intersect at common depots. In Fordham, Poe himself lived near a stop that had recently been added to the New York and Harlem line, one of the nation's earliest commuter trains, and he alluded in letters to living "about 14 miles from New-York along the Harlam Rail-Road" (L 792). Because of the uncoordinated patchwork nature of rail lines, travel even between major cities involved changeovers and, frequently, multiple modes of transportation. Steamboats, the more established alternative to horsepower, connected northeastern cities by way of rivers, canals, bays, and inlets. For instance, it was possible for Poe to travel between New York City and Providence by steamboat, but it was probably faster to combine modes of transport.[7] When he traveled home to Fordham from Providence on September 25, he took a late afternoon train to Stonington, Connecticut, where he caught a steamship that paddled its way overnight through Long Island Sound to Manhattan, made his way from an East River dock to a stop on the New York and Harlem line (probably in or near the Bowery), and rode for about an hour to get within walking distance of his rural cottage.[8] On another trip, he wrote to Helen Whitman from the steamboat: "It is 5 o'clock & the boat is just being made fast to the wharf. I shall start in the train that leaves New York at 7 for Fordham" (L 2:720).

Poe's letters to Helen Whitman reveal his desperate state of mind in the fall of 1848. A nine-page letter from October 18, between his first and second visits to Lowell, responds frantically to her having told him that she has heard numerous reports of his lacking principles or "moral sense." "Is it possible," Poe asks, "that such expressions as these could have been *repeated* to me—to me—by one whom I loved—ah, whom I *love*—by one at whose feet I knelt—I *still* kneel—in deeper worship than ever man offered to God?" (L 2:707) It's a manipulative letter: he has no wish but to die now that he knows she can't really love him; she is listening only to his worst enemies; and the class difference between them (*"you are comparatively rich while am poor"*) means that "the World" would never sanction their marriage. On November 26 he writes, "My sole hope, now, is *in you*, Helen. As you are true to me or fail me, so do I live or die" (L 2:734). On the next page Poe goes from abjection to promises of conquest, inviting Helen to share his publishing ambitions: "Would it *not* be 'glorious,' *darling*, to establish, in America, the sole unquestionable aristocracy—that of intellect—to secure its supremacy—to lead & to control it? All this I *can* do, Helen, & will—if you bid me—and aid me" (L 2:735).

It is hard to tell how much of this full-throttle pleading stems from Poe's histrionic nature and how much was a calculated attempt to access the "aid" to which he refers. Helen's family *was* well-off; she lived in a large colonial house on fashionable Benefit Street with her mother, Anna Marsh Power, who disliked Poe and suspected that he was after her daughter's money. Of course, Poe insisted that money was an obstacle rather than an incentive for him, and he was forced to back up that claim by signing a consent agreement acknowledging that Mrs. Power would now have sole legal control of the family estate. Aside from hoping that Helen's family money would still benefit him somehow, Poe had other reasons to want to marry her: she was attractive; she was compatible with him as a poet, freethinker, and mystic;

and she loved and admired him. Helen was concerned that he would be unhappy with her because she was older that he (by six years, to the day) and in fragile health, which included an inability to have sex (yes, she told him this). Poe assured her that none of that mattered.

What he didn't tell her was that he was in love with Annie Richmond. Back in Fordham on November 16, Poe wrote to Annie proclaiming his love in terms reminiscent of his letters to Helen, with slightly more tortured syntax: "So long as I think that you *know* I love you, as no man ever loved woman—so long as I think you comprehend in some measure, the fervor with which I adore you, *so* long, no worldly trouble can ever render me absolutely wretched." He calls her "my own sweet *sister* Annie, my *pure* beautiful angel—*wife* of my soul" (L 721). This emphasis on her being a sister, and pure (both words underscored by Poe, "sister" repeated three more times in this letter) while also his soul's *wife* acknowledges the unconsummatable nature of his desire. But it also recalls his relationship with his child bride Virginia, "Sissy," with whom he had no children, and who, like Annie, was much younger than himself.

But the letter's most intense drama lies in an incident related by Poe: he had recently tried to kill himself. If Poe is to be believed, he took the train from Providence to Boston, where he swallowed an ounce of laudanum, an elixir of opium dissolved in alcohol. His plan was to send for Annie, who would rush to his side as he swallowed another ounce, so he could die in her arms. His poem "For Annie," which he sent to her a few months later, is a fantasy of this attempted suicide:

When the light was extinguished
   She covered me warm,
And she prayed to the angels

To keep me from harm—
To the queen of the angels
To shield me from harm.

And I lie so composedly,
Now, in my bed,
(Knowing her love)
That you fancy me dead—
And I rest so contentedly,
Now in my bed,
(With her love at my breast)
That you fancy me dead—
That you shudder to look at me,
Thinking me dead:—

But my heart it is brighter
Than all of the many
Stars in the sky,
For it sparkles with Annie—
It glows with the light
Of the love of my Annie—
With the thought of the light
Of the eyes of my Annie. (P 458–59)

An ounce of laudanum might have been enough to kill Poe—
in fact, it impaired him to the point that he could not mail
the letter urging Annie to join him—but, he later told Annie,
"a friend was at hand, who aided & (if it can be called sav-
ing) saved me," probably by inducing vomiting. He then went
back to Providence and visited Helen Whitman again: "Here
I saw *her*, & spoke, for *your* sake, the words which you urged
me to speak"—surely words of devotion, as Annie was probably encouraging him to marry Helen (L 2:722).

So Poe trudged on in his pursuit of Helen Whitman as he
recovered from the laudanum overdose, and Helen agreed to

an engagement on the condition that he give up drinking entirely. Poe returned to Providence in late December to present a new lecture, "The Poetic Principle," and he and Helen began making wedding arrangements. But when she learned, during this visit, that Poe had broken his pledge to abstain from alcohol, she called it off. Poe's attempts to change her mind only made matters worse, and he finally stormed out of her mother's house, never to see her again. Two weeks later he expressed relief in a letter to Annie Richmond, adding that he had gotten back to work and "resolved to *get rich*—to triumph—for your sweet sake" (L 2:749).

He would not get rich, but Poe did resume his career as a magazinist in early 1849. After a long fiction-writing drought, he published five new stories, including the futuristic satire "Mellonta Tauta" and an unsettling tale of a court jester's revenge, "Hop-Frog." He sent what turned out to be his last four tales, as well as the new poems "For Annie," "To My Mother," and "Eldorado," to a cheap Boston weekly paper, *The Flag of Our Union*, because it paid promptly and reasonably well, and its editor would print whatever Poe gave him. He also sent a few poems, including then-unsold "Annabel Lee," to Rufus Griswold for a new edition of his *Poets and Poetry of America*. Meanwhile, Poe revived his "Marginalia" series for the *Southern Literary Messenger* and added a similar series called "Fifty Suggestions" in *Graham's*. In February, he reported to his old friend F. W. Thomas that "living buried in the country makes a man savage—wolfish. I am just in the humor for a fight." That Poe saw this rural "wolfishness" in positive terms is verified by his next lines: "You will be pleased to hear that I am in better health than I ever knew myself to be—full of energy and bent upon success" (L 2:771).

And yet, by May 1849, he was mired in depression. As he wrote to Annie Richmond, "I am full of dark forebodings.

Nothing cheers or comforts me. My life seems wasted—the future looks a dreary blank; but I will struggle on and 'hope against hope'" (L 2:796–97). Poe told Annie that his sadness was "unaccountable," suggesting an organic mood disorder. At the same time, he did have specific reasons for feeling defeated: he was barely getting by financially, he was in love with a married woman, and he was now more often mocked than celebrated by his contemporaries. In late 1848, his former friend James Russell Lowell had published *A Fable for Critics*, a popular pamphlet-length poem that satirized (sometimes gently, sometimes severely) the field of contemporary American writers. Lowell summed up Poe's reputation as a pedantic critic who might be too smart for his own good:

> There comes Poe with his Raven, like Barnaby Rudge,
> Three fifths of him genius and two fifths sheer fudge,
> Who talks like a book of iambs and pentameters,
> In a way to make people of common sense damn meters,
> Who has written some things quite the best of their kind,
> But the heart somehow seems all squeezed out by the mind.[9]

A few months later, *Holden's Dollar Magazine* (edited by Poe's embittered former partner C. F. Briggs) published the first installment of a similarly conceived satire by "Motley Manners, Esquire" titled "A Mirror for Authors," with a silhouette depicting Poe as a dancing "Indian" brandishing a tomahawk:

> With tomahawk upraised for deadly blow,
> Behold our literary Mohawk, Poe!
> Sworn tyrant he o'er all who sin in verse—
> His own the standard, damns he all that's worse;
> And surely not for this shall he be blamed—
> For worse than his deserves that it be damned!

Who can so well detect the plagiary's flaw?
"Set thief to catch thief" is an ancient saw.[10]

While these caricatures provide a sense of how Poe was seen late in his career, Lowell and "Motley Manners" (A.J.H. Duganne) restricted themselves to Poe's public persona as a poet/critic. Others, like Poe's recent antagonist John M. Daniel of the Richmond *Semi-Weekly Examiner*, took more personal shots: responding in January to the erroneous news that Poe and Helen Whitman were about to be married, Daniel wished the couple well before adding, "We also hope [Poe] will leave off getting drunk in restoratives, and keep his money in his pockets, except when he takes them out to pay his bills."[11]

If Poe was depressed in the spring of 1849, he also had a ray of hope, emanating from, of all places, Oquawka, Illinois. Edwin H. N. Patterson, the twenty-one-year-old editor of the *Oquawka Spectator*, had just come into a large inheritance, and had written to Poe offering to partner on a national magazine, under Poe's editorial control. Patterson's letter had been misdirected, so Poe received it some four months after it was sent, but he wrote back eagerly, explaining the delay and laying out his well-rehearsed formula for a successful five-dollar literary magazine. He then proposed "to take a tour through the principal States— especially West & South," lecturing to pay expenses and to drum up subscriptions (L 2:794). Later, the two men agreed to meet in St. Louis, Missouri, to finalize their plans at the conclusion of Poe's tour. Meanwhile, Patterson was to send fifty dollars to Richmond to defray his partner's expenses. Poe traveled once more to Lowell in late May to see Annie and solicit subscriptions; he planned to start the "tour" soon after returning to Fordham, but he lingered there until the end of June. He finally set out for Richmond on June 29, taking a steamboat to Perth Amboy, New Jersey, where he caught a train to Philadelphia.[12]

Poe arrived in Philadelphia as cholera was again sweeping through the city. Believing he had contracted the disease, he tried to counteract it by taking calomel, a mercury chloride mineral widely used as a purgative, which almost certainly made him sicker (L 2:828–29).[13] Whatever the cause, Poe's symptoms were not just physical. He wrote to Muddy that he had been "totally deranged," describing an attack of *mania-à-potu* (delirium tremens), though he also claimed not to have been drinking. He was jailed briefly in Moyamensing Prison in South Philadelphia, probably for drunkenness. He lost his valise, and when he found it (at the train depot) he discovered that his lectures were gone (L 2:824). John Sartain, an engraver and publisher whom Poe knew from his years in Philadelphia, later recalled a disturbing encounter during Poe's long, unscheduled stay in the city. Poe came to Sartain's studio seeking shelter, explaining that he had narrowly escaped being thrown from a train by men who were out to kill him. He had Sartain clip off his moustache with scissors to alter his appearance, and that night led his friend to Fairmount and the Schuylkill River, not far from where he had lived six years earlier. Sitting on the steps of the waterworks, Poe described horrific hallucinations he had recently experienced, in which he was forced to watch as his tormentors dismembered his beloved mother-in-law.[14] Eventually, with help from Sartain, George Lippard, and another friend, Chauncey Burr, Poe regained sufficient strength, sanity, and borrowed funds to complete his journey to Richmond.[15]

In Richmond, Poe gradually recovered from the hallucinogenic near-death experience of his two-week layover in Philadelphia. Upon his arrival on July 14, he stayed at the American Hotel on Main Street before moving to the Swan

Tavern, a boardinghouse on Broad Street, and later, less expensive lodgings at the Madison House on Tenth and Bank Streets, all in the center of town near the capitol, where Poe grew up, and where he, Muddy, and Virginia had lived throughout 1836.[16] Over the next two-plus months, he spent time at the homes of the Mackenzies, old family friends of the Allans and the foster family of his sister, Rosalie, and their neighbors the Talleys, in the western suburbs along Broad Street.[17] Just two years younger than her brother, Rosalie had stayed in Richmond, adopted by the Mackenzies, living the comfortable but constricted existence of an unmarried adult woman, her life prospects limited even more by some degree of intellectual disability. She and Edgar had not remained close, but during this extended visit "Rose" was often nearby, clinging to her brother's reflected celebrity, even delivering notes and manuscripts for him.[18] At Talevera, the home of the Talley family, Poe seems to have focused his attention on twenty-seven-year-old Susan Talley, who later recalled their relationship in an article for *Scribner's Magazine* and in her (otherwise unreliable) biography *The Home Life of Poe*. "He became the fashion" in Richmond, according to Talley, "and was *fêted* in society and discussed in the papers." He was asked to recite "The Raven" so often that her family tried to protect him by discouraging visitors from making the request.[19] Talley remembered Poe as charming and upbeat during most of that summer, although she also recalled two episodes when he was incapacitated for days due to heavy drinking.

It is unclear how much progress Poe was making enlisting subscribers for the *Stylus*; he was at least earning some money—and publicity—through lectures, but those earnings were barely enough to keep up with his expenses.[20] He continued to negotiate the terms of his partnership with Patterson but delayed the projected magazine launch from January to July of the following year. Meanwhile, having given up on finding an audience for *Eureka*, he gave three presentations on "The Poetic Principle," at the Exchange Hotel's Concert Room in Richmond on August 17 and September 24 and at Norfolk Academy on September 14. In this summation of his poetic theory, Poe refrained from trashing other poets or "talking like a book of iambs and pentameters"; he even recited, with admiration, Longfellow's "The Day Is Done." Instead of applying painstaking analysis, he pleased his audiences with lofty pronouncements: "I would define . . . the Poetry of words as *The Rhythmical Creation of Beauty*" (E 78); "while [the poetic] Principle itself is, strictly and simply, the Human Aspiration for Supernal Beauty, the manifestation of the Principle is always found in *an elevating excitement of the Soul*" (E 92–93). While in Norfolk for the lecture, he visited Old Point Comfort, where he had been stationed in the Army two decades before; now he recited poems—"Annabel Lee," "Ulalume," and, of course, "The Raven"—to an admiring group of young women in white dresses on the grounds of the waterfront Hygeia Hotel.[21]

Though not entirely healthy or consistently sober, Poe enjoyed a measure of stability that summer in Richmond, so it seemed like a good time to renew his pursuit of Elmira Royster Shelton, whom he had visited the previous year. The most significant obstacle, from Mrs. Shelton's perspective, was financial: as a stipulation of her husband's will, if she remarried she would lose control of the estate, along with three-fourths of "all profits and income."[22] And yet Poe seems to have won her over: on September 22, Elmira wrote to Maria Clemm, introducing herself in terms that indicate an impending marriage to Edgar. (On the other hand, she maintained long after Poe's death that there was no formal engagement and that she "[did] not think I should have mar-

Figure 5.1 Elmira Royster Shelton's house on Church Hill in Richmond, Virginia, where Poe visited her during his stay in 1849. Poe's mother, Eliza, is buried in St. John's Churchyard, across the street from the house.

ried him under any circumstances.")[23] Poe felt he needed the marriage but did not really want it. In an August 29 letter to Muddy, he professed his love to his mother-in-law and Annie Richmond, while providing detailed information about Elmira's income. On September 10, while at Old Point

Comfort, he told Muddy that "my heart sinks at the idea of this marriage. *I think*, however, that it will certainly take place & that immediately" (L 2: 836). But a week later, in a more sanguine mood, he wrote, "I think she loves me more devotedly than any one I ever knew & I cannot help loving her in return" (L 2: 837).

While vacillating on this potential marriage, Poe had received an offer from the husband of an aspiring poet, Marguerite St. Leon Loud of Philadelphia, to edit a volume of her poems for one hundred dollars. Broke as he was, Poe could hardly turn down the offer, so he planned to leave Richmond in the last week of September, stop in Philadelphia to work with the Louds, then proceed to New York and, presumably, accompany Maria back to Richmond. When Mrs. Shelton saw Poe the night of September 26, he was "very sad, and complained of being quite sick" and feverish. She was surprised to discover the next day that he had left on a steamboat for Baltimore, where he was to catch a train for Philadelphia.

Poe made it to Baltimore, but no further. Five days later, a printer named Joseph Walker discovered him in a tavern on East Lombard Street known variously as Ryan's, Gunnar's Hall, and the Fourth Ward Hotel, and wrote to Poe's friend Joseph Snodgrass describing "a gentleman, rather worse for wear . . . who appears in great distress, & says he is acquainted with you, and I assure you, he is in need of immediate assistance."[24] Poe was either unconscious or incoherent, and he was wearing clothes that did not fit him. What had happened during the previous five days remains a mystery. There is no evidence that Poe had planned to stay in Baltimore, but he must have encountered someone or something he hadn't expected: a worsening illness, an old acquaintance who insisted on a drink, possibly even a mugger or some other form of foul play. His cousin Neilson

Poe, who lived in Baltimore, believed Edgar had left for Philadelphia on a train, started drinking en route, and was conducted back to Baltimore in a state of delirium. A later theory seized on the fact that Ryan's was being used as a polling place on the day he was found there: had Poe been "cooped"—plied with alcohol and forced by partisan thugs to vote at various precincts?[25] Whatever the lost details, Poe had been ill upon his arrival in Baltimore and drank heavily in the days that followed. His springtime depression and his derangement a few months earlier in Philadelphia underscore the suggestion that he was suffering from neurological disease, possibly caused, or at least worsened, by alcohol.

Snodgrass came to the tavern and, along with Henry Herring, a relative of Poe's by marriage, helped convey Poe to Washington College Hospital, about a mile and a half away in the eastern part of the city. He lingered there, semiconscious, for another three days, and died on October 7. The year before, Poe had tried to die in the city where he was born; instead, he died in the city where he had found a career and a family. But, in light of his peripatetic life, the location of his death seems less significant than the fact that he died "on the road." Appropriately, the journey he had begun should have taken him to each of the four cities that shaped his career and where he lived most of that life: leaving Richmond, bound for New York by way of Baltimore and Philadelphia. Like so much of his life, though, this trip didn't go as planned.

Poe was buried on October 9, in a Presbyterian graveyard in central Baltimore. The weather was cold, and only about eight mourners attended—Snodgrass, Neilson Poe, and Henry Herring among them. One can only speculate, but it seems likely that if Poe had died in Richmond, where he had recently enjoyed some celebrity and reconnected with old acquaintances, his funeral would have been better attended;

Figure 5.2 The building where Poe died in Baltimore, Maryland, known as Washington University Hospital at the time.

even in New York, despite the scandals of the past few years, he would have drawn mourners from the literary and publishing world. But, over time, the fact that Poe died in Baltimore would allow that city to claim him in a way that no other "Poe place" has quite matched.

It took a while, partly because Poe's reputation was clouded by the work of his own literary executor, his sometime rival and successor at *Graham's Magazine*, Rufus Griswold. In a long obituary published in the New York *Tribune* and in a longer memoir included in Poe's collected works, Griswold exaggerated Poe's faults and fabricated a few incidents to depict his subject as thoroughly selfish, dishonest, and unstable. At the same time, Griswold consistently attested to Poe's literary genius, and his edition made the magnitude of Poe's achievement clearer than it had been during his lifetime. Griswold's characterization and the responses it elicited framed all discussion of Poe's work well into the twentieth century (and to some extent, into the twenty-first), creating a mystique and a narrative of controversy that have helped sustain interest in his poetry and fiction ever since.

Poe attracted many defenders in the long aftermath of Griswold's defamations, and, in a sense, the city of Baltimore became one of his most prominent advocates. In 1865 the Public School Teachers' Association took the lead in fundraising for a suitable monument to redeem Poe's unmarked grave; a memorial committee took over the project several years later and eventually raised sufficient funds to commission an eight-foot marble and granite monument. In 1875 his remains were moved to a more prominent location on the grounds where the new marker was erected near the corner of West Fayette and North Greene Streets—a destination for Poe pilgrims and, from about 1949 to 2009, a mysterious visitor known as the "Poe Toaster," who left a tribute of cognac and roses each year on Poe's birthday, slipping in under cover of darkness. The occasion of the reinterment was marked with speeches, choral performances, and the reading of letters from poets and dignitaries. Though he was not asked to speak, Walt Whitman was among the attendees.

In the decades following his reinterment, Poe was canonized in every American city where he had lived. In 1885, a memorial commissioned by a society of New York actors, featuring a marble female figure placing a wreath around a bronze bust of Poe, was dedicated at the Metropolitan

Museum of Art. On the fiftieth anniversary of Poe's death, the University of Virginia unveiled a bust of Poe that still adorns the reading room of the main library; reporting on the event, the *New York Times* noted that the depiction of Poe by sculptor Julian Zolnay "is an intellectual man in a state of dejection. . . . It is not the Poe of Griswold."[26] Baltimore, Richmond, and Charlottesville held centenary celebrations of Poe's birth in 1909; around the same time, Richmonders formed a Poe Memorial Association and began raising funds to enshrine Poe on the city's Monument Avenue. Their efforts to place Poe among the procession of Confederate generals fell short, but the association later reformed under the leadership of Poe collector James H. Whitty to establish the Poe Shrine in 1922, which evolved into what is now Richmond's Poe Museum.[27] Meanwhile, New York City purchased the Fordham cottage, moving it a short distance to the newly dedicated "Poe Park" in 1913, where it still stands.[28] Poe's last residence in Philadelphia was purchased by department store magnate and Poe aficionado Richard Gimbel in the 1930s; having established it as a museum, Gimbel bequeathed the property to the National Park Service in 1978.[29] In the same year Poe Park was established in the Bronx, Boston renamed the intersection near his birthplace, Broadway and Carver Street, "Poe Place"; a century later, the city would dedicate Stefanie Rocknak's life-sized statue "Poe Returning to Boston" nearby at the corner of Boylston and Charles Streets.

Rocknak's Boston statue may capture Poe better than any other single image: in full stride, on a busy city street, returning to Boston, or possibly leaving, or—if we imagine the same statue on a street in Richmond, Philadelphia, or New York—staying a step or two ahead of his last landlord. As much as Poe seems to have preferred living in the semiru-

Figure 5.3 Stefanie Rocknak's sculpture *Poe Returning to Boston* stands at the corner of Boylston Street and Charles Street South, near the site of Poe's birth.

ral outskirts, he was very much a city creature, participating in a period of rapid urban development. His career as a magazinist was a product of that development: he not only wrote for but worked in various editorial roles in magazine offices located in the centers of Richmond, Philadelphia, and New York. His unrealized dream of artistic and editorial self-sufficiency was to control one of those offices. He made city life part of his fiction, incorporating mystery, pestilence, con artists, violence, and alienation into urban tales such as "The Man of the Crowd," the Dupin trilogy, "The Business-Man," "King Pest," "The Man That Was Used Up," and "Some Words with a Mummy." As a journalist and critic, he surveyed New York City in "Doings of Gotham" and its prominent writers in "The Literati of New York City." Moreover, spending his life on the move, between or within cities, Poe became essentially cosmopolitan in his outlook, arguably America's first modern writer.

In his landmark 1925 book *In the American Grain*, the poet William Carlos Williams asserted that Poe was "a genius intimately shaped by his locality and time. . . . It is the

New World, or to leave that for a better term, it is a *new locality* that is in Poe assertive; it is America, the first great burst through to expression of a re-awakened genius of *place*." But Williams makes clear that Poe's new American "locality" is no single region or town—he "founded" American literature by clearing the ground and sweeping away "colonial imitation": "What he wanted was connected with no particular place; therefore it must be *where* he *was*."[30] Indeed—and he was, invariably, as Rocknak depicts him, on the move, whether the city was Boston, New York, Philadelphia, Baltimore, or Richmond. The statue suggests that he packed in a hurry: Poe is leaving a trail of manuscripts (and a human heart!) spilling out of his unclosed suitcase. Also emerging from the case is a very large raven, his own symbol of grief and loss but here also a symbol of his achievement and fame, accomplished even though, or maybe because, he had to keep moving.

Acknowledgments

This book would not have been possible without the work of countless Poe scholars and biographers, including those who came before and many whom I am fortunate to call friends. The heroic biographical work of Mary E. Phillips, Arthur Hobson Quinn, David K. Jackson, Dwight Thomas, and Kenneth Silverman gave *The Man of the Crowd* its foundation. Books such as *The American Face of Edgar Allan Poe*, edited by Shawn Rosenheim and Stephen Rachman, *Romancing the Shadow: Poe and Race*, edited by J. Gerald Kennedy and Liliane Weissberg, and *Edgar Allan Poe and the Masses* by Terence Whalen put Poe into meaningful conversation with nineteenth-century American culture, and I drew heavily from those volumes (among many others) in these pages. I am especially grateful to Jeffrey Savoye, who maintains the indispensible Poe Society of Baltimore website: eapoe.org. I learned about and accessed many of the historical texts cited in this book through the Poe Society website. In 2014, Philip Phillips invited me to Middle Tennessee State University to give a talk on Poe and Place; that visit, along with encouragement and advice from my colleague Joseph Kelly, got me moving on this project. Julia Eichelberger and Ellen Claire Lamb offered generous, helpful guidance on the manuscript and ongoing support. I would also like to acknowledge the journal *Poe Studies*, where some portions of chapter 4 previously appeared.

Michelle and I would also like to thank the College of Charleston for providing grants for this project on two occasions, and the English and Studio Art departments for additional support. Chris Semtner and Jaime Fawcett at the Poe Museum were unfailingly generous and helpful in our

Figure 6.1 Poe daguerreotype, 1848. (Daguerreotype is from the collection of the Poe Museum, Richmond, Virginia.)

visits to Richmond. We are forever grateful to our tireless agent, Jacqueline Flynn, for getting us here; to Anne Savarese at Princeton University Press, for her guidance; and to Emily Shelton, for her careful editing. Finally, we would like to express our love and thanks to Nancy Peeples and Mark Sloan, who lived with this book for the past six years.

Notes

Introduction: No Place Like Home

1. Arthur Hobson Quinn, *Edgar Allan Poe: A Critical Biography* (Baltimore: Johns Hopkins University Press, [1941] 1998), 719.

2. Bridget Bennett, "Home Songs and the Melodramatic Imagination: From 'Home, Sweet Home' to *The Birth of a Nation*," *Journal of American Studies* 46, no. 1 (2012): 171–87, quoted from 178.

3. Daniel Walker Howe, *What Hath God Wrought: The Transformation of America, 1815–1848* (New York: Oxford, 2007), 526.

4. James M. Volo and Dorothy Denneen Volo, *The Antebellum Period* (Westport, CT: Greenwood, 2004), 4.

5. Yi-Fu Tuan, *Space and Place: The Perspective of Experience* (Minneapolis: University of Minnesota Press, 1977), 149.

6. One notable exception in writing for nonspecialists about Poe is Jill Lepore's *New Yorker* essay "The Humbug" (2009), which was included in her book *The Story of America* (Princeton, NJ: Princeton University Press, 2012), 178–96. Lepore asserts that Poe "did not live out of time. He lived in hard times, dark times, up and down times" (180).

7. W. H. Auden, "Introduction" [*Edgar Allan Poe: Selected Prose and Poetry*, 1950], reprinted in *The Recognition of Edgar Allan Poe*, edited by Eric W. Carlson (Ann Arbor: University of Michigan Press, 1966), 221.

8. Richard Wilbur, "The House of Poe," in *Recognition of Edgar Allan Poe*, 258; my italics.

9. *Voices and Visions: Walt Whitman* (film), New York Center for Visual History, Annenberg/CPB Collection, 1988.

10. See Karen Halttunen, *Confidence Men and Painted Women: A Study of Middle-Class Culture in America, 1830–1870* (New Haven, CT: Yale University Press, 1982), especially chapter 2, "Hypocrisy and Sincerity in the World of Strangers" (33–55).

11. When he republished the story three years later in a collection of his tales, Poe covered his tracks by adding references that include the possibility of "a fatal accident under the roof of Madame Deluc" (the Parisian equivalent of Frederika Loss). See John E. Walsh, *Poe the Detective: The Mysterious Circumstances behind The Mystery of Marie Roget* (New Brunswick, NJ: Rutgers University Press, 1967); and Amy Gilman Srebnick, *The Mysterious Death of Mary Rogers:*

Sex and Culture in Nineteenth-Century New York (New York: Oxford University Press, 1997).

12. Brian Nicol, "The Urban Environment," in *Edgar Allan Poe in Context*, edited by Kevin J. Hayes (Cambridge: Cambridge University Press, 2013), 82.

Chapter 1: Richmond (1809–1827)

1. Kenneth Silverman, *Edgar A. Poe: Mournful and Never-ending Remembrance* (New York: HarperCollins, 1991), 6–7.

2. Dwight Thomas and David K. Jackson, *The Poe Log: A Documentary Life of Edgar Allan Poe, 1809–1849* (Boston: G. K. Hall, 1987), 15.

3. Campbell Gibson, "Population of the 100 Largest Cities and Other Urban Places in the United States: 1790 to 1990," US Census Bureau, https://www.census.gov/population/www/documentation /twps0027/ twps0027.html (accessed June 8, 2016).

4. Quoted in Agnes M. Bondurant, *Poe's Richmond* (Richmond, VA: Poe Associates, [1942] 1978), 7.

5. Maurice Duke and Daniel P. Jordan, eds., *A Richmond Reader, 1733–1883* (Chapel Hill: University of North Carolina Press, 1983), 88.

6. Bondurant, 16.

7. Bondurant, 198–99.

8. Silverman, 12 Bondurant, 196–97.

9. Mary E. Phillips, *Edgar Allan Poe the Man*, 2 vols. (Chicago: John C. Winston, 1926), 104; Christopher P. Semtner, *Edgar Allan Poe's Richmond: The Raven in the River City* (Charleston, SC: History, 2012), 28.

10. J. Gerald Kennedy, "The Realm of Dream and Memory: Poe's England," in *Poe and Place*, edited by Philip Edward Phillips (Cham, Switzerland: Palgrave, 2018), 73–74.

11. See Kennedy, "Realm of Dream and Memory," 71–96. See also Roy Porter, *London: A Social History* (Cambridge, MA: Harvard University Press, 1995), 185–86.

12. *The Complete Works and Letters of Charles Lamb* (New York: Modern Library, 1963), 687.

13. Tim Hitchcock, Robert Shoemaker, Clive Emsley, Sharon Howard, and Jamie McLaughlin, "A Population History of London," Old Bailey Proceedings Online, 1674–1913, version 7.0, March 018, www.oldbaileyonline.org (accessed March 29, 2019).

14. Kennedy, "Realm of Dream and Memory," 74. See also Heather Shore, "Mean Streets: Criminality, Immorality, and the Street in Early

Nineteenth-Century London," in *The Streets of London: From the Great Fire to the Great Stink*, edited by Tim Hitchcock and Heather Shore (London: Rivers Oram, 2003), 151–64.

15. *The Poetical Works of Shelley*, edited by Ford F. Newell (Boston: Houghton Mifflin, 1974), 262.

16. See Porter, 257–78.

17. On the debt of "The Man of the Crowd" to Dickens, see Stephen Rachman, "'Es lässt sich nicht schreiben': Plagiarism and 'The Man of the Crowd,'" in *The American Face of Edgar Allan Poe*, edited by Shawn Rosenheim and Stephen Rachman (Baltimore: Johns Hopkins University Press, 1995), 49–87.

18. Killis Campbell, "New Notes on Poe's Early Years," *Dial* 60 (February 17, 1916): 144 (accessed at www.eapoe.org).

19. Kennedy, "Realm of Dream and Memory," 86–89.

20. Thomas and Jackson, 26, 31, 42.

21. Eugene L. Dider, *Life of Edgar A. Poe* (New York: W. J. Widdleton, 1877), 30–31 (accessed at www.eapoe.org).

22. J. T. L. Preston, quoted in Silverman, 24.

23. Semtner, *Edgar Allan Poe's Richmond*, 36.

24. David K. Jackson, *Poe and the* Southern Literary Messenger (New York: Haskell House, [1934] 1970), 41.

25. Didier, 33–34.

26. Silverman, 25.

27. Thomas H. Ellis, "Edgar Allan Poe," *Richmond Standard*, May 7, 1881, 2 (accessed at www.eapoe.org). See also Semtner, *Edgar Allan Poe's Richmond*, 27.

28. Virginius Dabney, *Richmond: The Story of a City* (Charlottesville: University of Virginia Press, 1990), 92.

29. Keshia A. Case and Christopher P. Semtner, *Poe in Richmond* (Charleston, SC: Arcadia, 2009), 16.

30. Bondurant, 51; Christopher P. Semtner, "Poe's Richmond and Richmond's Poe," in Phillips, *Poe and Place*, 48.

31. Thomas and Jackson, 61.

32. Silverman, 28.

33. Semtner, "Poe's Richmond and Richmond's Poe," 44.

34. Biographer Hervey Allen asserted that Ellis and Allan were "not above trading in . . . old slaves whom they hired out at the coal pits until they died." See *Israfel: The Life and Times of Edgar Allan Poe*, rev. ed. (New York: Farrar & Rinehart, [1926] 1934), 27.

35. Thomas and Jackson, 24.

36. Marie Tyler-McGraw and Gregg D. Kimball, *In Bondage and Freedom: Antebellum Black Life in Richmond, Virginia* (Chapel Hill: University of North Carolina Press, 1988), 62. See also J. Gerald

Kennedy, "'Trust No Man': Poe, Douglass, and the Culture of Slavery," in *Romancing the Shadow: Poe and Race*, edited by J. Gerald Kennedy and Liliane Weissberg (New York: Oxford University Press, 2001), 227–57.

37. Henry Watson, *Narrative of Henry Watson, A Fugitive Slave* (Boston: Bela Marsh, 1850), 10–12.

38. Thomas and Jackson, 68.

39. Silverman, 31.

40. Thomas and Jackson, 69–70.

41. Silverman, 34.

42. Semtner, *Edgar Allan Poe's Richmond*, 54.

43. Quoted in Semtner, *Edgar Allan Poe's Richmond*, 58. Mary E. Phillips, in *Edgar Allan Poe the Man*, suggests that Allan confided to Elmira's father James Royster that Poe would not inherit any of his property, effectively colluding to block the marriage (226–27). See also Hervey Allen and Thomas Ollive Mabbott, "Introduction," in *Poe's Brother: The Poems of William Henry Leonard Poe* (New York: George H. Doran, 1926), 29–30 (accessed at www.eapoe.org).

44. Allen and Mabbott, 30–31; Thomas Ollive Mabbott, "Introduction," in *Merlin (Baltimore, 1827); Together with Recollections of Edgar A. Poe* (New York: Scholars' Facsimilies & Reprints, 1941), xiii–xvi.

45. See Silverman, 35, on the resemblance of Poe's letter to the Declaration of Independence.

46. Silverman, 9.

Chapter 2: Baltimore (1827–1838)

1. Robert Adger Law, "A Source for 'Annabel Lee,'" *Journal of English and Germanic Philology* 21 (1922): 341–46. See also Scott Peeples, "Unburied Treasure: Edgar Allan Poe in the South Carolina Lowcountry," with photographs by Michelle Van Parys, *Southern Cultures* 22, no. 2 (Summer 2016): 5–22.

2. Silverman, 42–43.

3. See William Hecker, "Introduction," in *Private Perry and Mister Poe: The West Point Poems, 1831*, edited by William Hecker (Baton Rouge: Louisiana State University Press, 2005), xvii–lxxv.

4. Silverman, 63.

5. Silverman, 69.

6. Camilla Townsend, *Tales of Two Cities: Race and Economic Culture in Early Republican North and South America* (Austin: University of Texas Press, 2000), 33.

7. Townsend, 41.

8. Gary Lawson Browne, *Baltimore in the Nation, 1790–1861* (Chapel Hill: University of North Carolina Press, 1980), 86; Townsend, 38.

9. Campbell Gibson, "Popluation of the 100 Largest Cities and Other Urban Places in the United States: 1790 to 1990," U. S. Census Bureau, June 1998, https://www.census.gov/population/www/documen tation/twps0027/twps0027.html (accessed September 25, 2019); Seth Rockman, *Scraping By: Wage Labor, Slavery, and Survival in Early Baltimore* (Baltimore: Johns Hopkins University Press, 2009), 43, 31.

10. Rockman, 26, 168.

11. Rockman, 34.

12. Mary Ellen Hayward and Frank R. Shivers Jr., eds., *The Architecture of Baltimore: An Illustrated History* (Baltimore: Johns Hopkins University Press, 2004), 80.

13. Hayward and Shivers, 83.

14. Lawrence C. Wroth, "Poe's Baltimore," *Johns Hopkins Alumni Magazine* 17, no. 4 (June 1929), 303–4.

15. Frances Trollope, *Domestic Manners of the Americans* (1832), edited by John Lauritz Larson (St. James, NY: Brandywine, 1993), 108–9.

16. Wroth, 303.

17. John H. Hewitt, *Shadows on the Wall; or Glimpses of the Past* (Baltimore: Turnbull Brothers, 1877), 133.

18. *A Detailed and Correct Account of the Grand Civic Procession, in the City of Baltimore, on the Fourth of July, 1828; in Honor of the Day, and in Commemoration of the Commencement of the Baltimore and Ohio Rail-Road* (Baltimore: Thomas Murphy, 1828), 43. The song is also quoted by Rockman, 16.

19. Rockman, 158–93.

20. Mary Markey and Dean Krimmel, "Poe's Mystery House: The Search for Mechanics Row," *Maryland Historical Magazine* 84, no. 4 (1991): 389–90.

21. David F. Gaylin, *Edgar Allan Poe's Baltimore* (Charleston, SC: Arcadia), 34.

22. Markey and Krimmel, 392.

23. Markey and Krimmel, 392.

24. John C. Miller, "Did Edgar Allan Poe Really Sell a Slave?" *Poe Studies/Dark Romanticism* 9, no. 2 (1976): 52–53.

25. See Rockman, 57–61, on term slavery in Baltimore.

26. Markey and Krimmel, 394.

27. See Kennedy, "'Trust No Man': Poe, Douglass, and the Culture of Slavery." Townsend uses Bailey/Douglass as a "guide" to 1830s Baltimore (33–46).

28. Silverman, 84–85.

29. Rockman, 185–86.

30. Biographers have hedged on whether Poe was actually jailed, acknowledging the lack of legal records to corroborate what he and Maria told Allan. I find the story credible: while one cannot rule out the possibility that Poe and Maria Clemm were simply lying to John Allan to play on his sympathy, that sort of outright fraud seems unnecessarily risky, especially if Poe had reason to expect that he might again need Allan's help in the future. The fact that Allan asked a third party in Baltimore, John Walsh, to liberate Poe is an indication of how easily such a fraud could have been exposed.

31. Silverman, 96.

32. See Leon Jackson, *The Business of Letters: Authorial Economies in Antebellum America* (Stanford, CA: Stanford University Press, 2008), 186–234, on literary competitions and Poe's involvement with them, discussed specifically on 218–30.

33. John Earle Uhler, "Literary Taste and Culture in Baltimore: A Study of the Periodical Literature of Baltimore from 1815 to 1833," PhD diss., Johns Hopkins University, 1927, 7.

34. Uhler, 119, 133, 204; Floyd Stovall, *Edgar Poe the Poet: Essays New and Old on the Man and His Work* (Charlottesville: University of Virginia Press, 1969), 42–43. See also Jeffrey A. Savoye, "Poe and Baltimore: Crossroads and Redemption," in Phillips, *Poe and Place*, 103.

35. The story was first printed in an early Poe biography, William Fearing Gill's *Life of Edgar Allan Poe* (New York: Appleton, 1877), 46–49. Gill attributes it to a "Baltimore acquaintance" of Poe. See also Mary E. Phillips, who picked up the story, with some differences, from a biography of Lofland (*Edgar Allan Poe the Man* 1:461). Thomas Ollive Mabbott surmises that the story has "some basis in fact" (P 502).

36. Quoted from Stovall, 70. Stovall explicates "The Musiad" at length and conjectures that Poe wrote it himself, but Mabbott and other editors have not accepted the poem as Poe's.

37. Stovall, 84–85.

38. John C. French, "Poe's Literary Baltimore," *Maryland Historical Magazine* 32, no. 2 (1937): 101–12; French provides details about the Delphian Club and its resemblance to Poe's Folio Club on 109–12. See also Alexander Hammond, "Edgar Allan Poe's *Tales of the Folio Club*: The Evolution of a Lost Book," in *Poe at Work: Seven Textual Studies*, edited by Benjamin Franklin Fisher IV (Baltimore: Edgar Allan Poe Society, 1978), 13–43.

39. Thomas and Jackson, 134.

40. Although "Shadow—A Parable" was not published until 1835, Mabbott believes it was written before May 1833, as a companion piece to "Silence" ("Siope"), which was one of the eleven 1833 Folio Club tales (P 188).

41. Townsend, 35.

42. Thomas and Jackson, 142–43.

43. Augustus Van Cleef, "Poe's Mary," *Harper's New Monthly Magazine*, March 1889, 686 (accessed at www.eapoe.org). In his landmark 1941 biography, Arthur Hobson Quinn dismissed Starr's account altogether, but on largely sexist grounds: "If there is any form of evidence that is fundamentally unreliable, it is that of an elderly woman concerning her youthful love affair with a man who has since become famous" (196). Quinn also claimed that Starr's description of Poe as atheistic and disrespectful of women and marriage was at odds with other accounts of his behavior, which is true to an extent. But Poe was never religiously devout; in fact, his unconventional views of the nature of God and the universe would later scare away his companion Marie Louise Shew. He does come across as more coarse in his treatment of Starr than he would with other women, but his behavior toward Starr while intoxicated is not out of character; in fact, it somewhat parallels the circumstances of his falling-out with Sarah Helen Whitman in 1848. Mabbott and Silverman both credit the "outline" of Starr's account but are suspicious of at least some of the particulars. Poe's friend F. W. Thomas, in notes published by early Poe scholar James Whitty, recounted a conversation with one James Tuhey, who claimed to have known Poe in the early 1830s and recalled that he had wanted to marry "Miss Deveraux, a dark-eyed beauty, whose parents came from Ireland." Tuhey told Thomas that because of her young age, Mary's parents, "with the Cairnes" [Poe's grandmother and Maria Clemm], interfered and broke off the affair" (Whitty, "Memoir," in *The Complete Poems of EAP* [Boston: Houghton Mifflin, 1911], xxxiv.) Tuhey's recollections of Poe are otherwise highly suspect and are rarely referenced in Poe biographies, but they do provide corroboration for Poe wanting to marry Mary Devereux. Since Thomas died in 1866, neither he nor Tuhey could have picked up that piece of information from the Van Cleef interview published in 1889.

44. There is a secondhand report, from a West Point classmate, of Poe working in a brickyard in Baltimore in 1834: Robert T. P. Allen, "Edgar Allan Poe," *Scribner's Monthly*, September 1875, 143 (accessed at www.eapoe.org).

45. Lambert A. Wilmer, "Recollections of Edgar A. Poe," *Baltimore Daily Commercial*, May 23, 1866, 1 (accessed at www.eapoe.org).

46. Van Cleef, 635.

47. Wilmer, 1.

48. Gaylin, 44.

49. Wilmer, 1.

50. Thomas and Jackson, 148.

51. Thomas and Jackson, 149.

52. Silverman, 107. See also Michael R. Haines, "Long Term Marriage Patterns in the United States from Colonial Times to the Present," National Bureau of Economic Research (NBER) Working Paper Series on Historical Factors in Long Run Growth, no. 80, 1996, National Bureau of Economic Research, Cambridge, Massachusetts, https://www.nber.org/papers/h0080 (accessed March 10, 2020). Citing the work of Warren C. Sanderson, Haines places the average age of first marriage for white women at twenty in 1830.

53. N. H. Morrison, a friend of Neilson Poe, told early Poe biographer John Henry Ingram, "To prevent so premature a marriage, Nelson [sic] Poe offered to take the young lady, his half-sister-in-law, into his own family, educate her, & take care of her—-with the understanding that, if, after a few years, the two young people should feel the same towards each other, they should be married" (John Carl Miller, *Building Poe Biography* [Baton Rouge: Louisiana State University Press, 1977], 52). Burton R. Pollin argued that it was Maria Clemm who most needed to keep the family together in the face of Neilson Poe's offer, and that she manipulated Poe into marrying Virginia. See Pollin, "Maria Clemm, Poe's Aunt: His Boon or His Bane?" *Mississippi Quarterly* 48, no. 2 (1995): 211–24.

54. Savoye, 100.

55. Thomas and Jackson, 175.

56. Thomas and Jackson, 192.

57. Terence Whalen, *Edgar Allan Poe and the Masses: The Political Economy of Literature in Antebellum America* (Princeton, NJ: Princeton University Press, 1999), 65–66. Whalen discusses the history and effects of the exaggerated circulation figures throughout chapter 3 ("Fables of Circulation: Poe's Influence on the *Messenger*"), 58–75.

58. Silverman, 108.

59. Thomas and Jackson, 242.

60. Quinn, 267.

61. Edwin G. Burrows and Mike Wallace, *Gotham: A History of New York City to 1898* (New York: Oxford University Press, 1999), 611–14.

Chapter 3: Philadelphia (1838–1844)

1. Quoted in Alasdair Roberts, *America's First Great Depression: Economic Crisis and Political Disorder after the Panic of 1837* (Ithaca, NY: Cornell University Press, 2012), 17.

2. Sam Bass Warner, *The Private City: Philadelphia in Three Periods of Its Growth*, rev. ed. (Philadelphia: University of Pennsylvania Press, [1968] 1987), 50–51. See also Elizabeth M. Geffen, "Industrial Development and Social Crisis, 1841–1854," in *Philadelphia: A 300-Year History*, edited by Russell F. Weigley (New York: Norton, 1982), 309.

3. See Nicholas B. Wainwright, "The Age of Nicholas Biddle, 1825–1841," in Weigley, *Philadelphia*, 265–69 and 275–77.

4. Edgar P. Richardson, "The Athens of America, 1800–1825," in Weigley, *Philadelphia*, 230.

5. Wainwright, 281–85.

6. Charles Dickens, *American Notes* (New York: Penguin, [1842] 2000), 110. See Samuel Otter, *Philadelphia Stories: America's Literature of Race and Freedom* (New York: Oxford University Press, 2010), 13.

7. Geffen, 307–8.

8. Michael Feldberg, "Urbanization as a Cause of Violence: Philadelphia as a Test Case," in *The Peoples of Philadelphia: A History of Ethnic Groups and Lower-Class Life, 1790–1940*, edited by Allen F. Davis and Mark H. Haller (Philadelphia: University of Pennsylvania Press, [1973] 1998), 53–69. David Johnson reports that a survey of a single newspaper from 1836–78 "uncovered fifty-two gangs which were identified by name" (also in *Peoples of Philadelphia*, 97).

9. Otter, 135.

10. Geffen, 315.

11. Quoted in Geffen, 318.

12. See Otter, 165–80; David S. Reynolds, Introduction to *The Quaker City; or, The Monks of Monk Hall*, by George Lippard, edited by David S. Reynolds (Amherst: University of Massachusetts Press, 1995), vii–xli; and Scott Peeples, "The City Mystery Novel," in *The Oxford History of the Novel in English, Vol. 5: The American Novel to 1870*, edited by J. Gerald Kennedy and Leland S. Person (New York: Oxford University Press, 2014), 548–63.

13. Dwight Rembert Thomas documents the evidence for these locations in "Poe in Philadelphia, 1838–1844: A Documentary Record," PhD diss., University of Pennsylvania, 1978, 13, 25–27, 825–28 (accessed at www.eapoe.org). Sixteenth Street was called "Schuylkill Seventh" when Poe lived there.

14. Wainwright, 281.

15. Heinzen, 27–28.

16. Nancy M. Heinzen, *The Perfect Square: A History of Rittenhouse Square* (Philadelphia: Temple University Press, 2009), 24.

17. Anne Clarke's reminiscence is quoted in the engraver John Sartain's memoir *The Reminiscences of a Very Old Man* (New York: Appleton, 1899), 216–17. Harris's article was published in *Hearth and Home*, January 9, 1875, 24 (accessed at www.eapoe.org).

18. Wainwright, 300.

19. Over the course of his career, Poe published seven tales, a number of book reviews, and the series "The Literati of New York City" in *Godey's*; however, he did not publish in *Godey's* while in Philadelphia, with the exception of "A Tale of the Ragged Mountains" in April 1844, the month he left for New York. For a detailed description of Poe's likely walk across town to the Burton's office, see Amy Branam Armiento, "Poe in Philadelphia," in *Poe Places*, edited by Philip Edward Phillips (Cham, Switzerland: Palgrave, 2018), 125.

20. Sartain, 224; Thomas, 353–57.

21. Heather A. Haveman, *Magazines and the Making of America: Modernization, Community, and Print Culture, 1741–1860* (Princeton, NJ: Princeton University Press, 2015),75.

22. Isabelle Lehuu, *Carnival on the Page: Popular Print Media in Antebellum America* (Chapel Hill: University of North Carolina Press, 2000), 26; Susan Belasco Smith and Kenneth M. Price, "Introduction," in *Periodical Literature in Nineteenth-Century America* (Charlottesville: University of Virginia Press, 1995), 6. See also Lyn H. Lofland, *A World of Strangers: Order and Action in Urban Public Space* (New York: Basic Books, 1973).

23. Haveman, 57–61, 26.

24. Haveman, 27.

25. Haveman, 31. See also Susan Belasco, "The Cultural Work of National Magazines," in *A History of the Book in America, Vol. 3: The Industrial Book, 1840–1880*, edited by Scott E. Casper, Jeffrey D. Groves, Stephen W. Nissenbaum, and Michael Winship (Chapel Hill: University of North Carolina Press, 2007), 258–70.

26. See Mabbott's notes in T 1:391; also Armiento, 129.

27. Thomas and Jackson, 297–98.

28. Thomas and Jackson, 312.

29. Thomas and Jackson, 318–19.

30. See John Ward Ostrom, "Edgar A. Poe: His Income as a Literary Entrepreneur," *Poe Studies* 15, no. 1 (1982): 1–7.

31. An analysis of prices by the website 24/7 Wall St. in 2010 provides an estimate similar to that of the Bureau of Labor Statistics. See Charles B. Stockdale, Michael B. Sauter, and Douglas A. McIntyre,

"A History of What Things Cost in America: 1776 to Today," 24/7 Wall St., September 26, 2010, http://247wallst.com/investing/2010 /09/16/the-history-of-what-things-cost-in-america-1776-to-today/ (accessed January 12, 2018).

32. Geffen, 335.

33. Robert L. Gale, *A Henry Wadsworth Longfellow Companion* (Westport, CT: Greenwood, 2003), 119.

34. For a nuanced discussion of the economies of writing during Poe's time, see Leon Jackson, *The Business of Letters: Authorial Economies in Antebellum America* (Stanford, CA: Stanford University Press, 2008).

35. Thomas, 73, 90.

36. Thomas and Jackson, 409; Mabbott's introduction to "The Gold-Bug," T 2:803.

37. Whalen, 197.

38. Whalen, 216–24; Marc Shell, *Money, Language, and Thought: Literary and Philosophical Economies from the Medieval to the Modern Era* (Berkeley: University of California Press, 1982), 5–23; J. Gerald Kennedy, *Strange Nation: Literary Nationalism and Cultural Conflict in the Age of Poe* (New York: Oxford University Press, 2016), 370–74.

39. *Poe's Contributions to Alexander's Weekly Messenger*, edited by Clarence S. Brigham (Worcester, MA: American Antiquarian Society, 1943), 37.

40. Karen Halttunen, *Confidence Men and Painted Women: A Study of Middle-Class Culture in America, 1830–1870* (New Haven, CT: Yale University Press, 1982), 1–32; and David M. Henkin, *City Reading: Written Words and Public Spaces in Antebellum New York* (New York: Columbia University Press, 1998).

41. In his introduction to "The Murders in the Rue Morgue," T. O. Mabbott writes that "it may not be the first detective story, but it is the first story deliberately written as such to attain worldwide popularity" (T 1:521).

42. Amy Gilman, "Edgar Allan Poe Detecting the City," in *The Mythmaking Frame of Mind: Social Imagination in American Culture*, edited by James Gilbert, Amy Gilman, Donald M. Scott, and Joan M. Scott (Belmont, CA: Wadsworth, 1993), 73.

43. See Gilman, 77.

44. Thomas, 57–58.

45. Thomas, 118–19.

46. See, for instance, Winthrop Jordan, *The White Man's Burden: Historical Origins of Racism in the United States* (New York: Oxford University Press, 1974), 15.

47. On the inevitability of racial subtext of "Rue Morgue" and reader participation in the story's meaning, see Ed White, "The Ourang-Outang Situation," *College Literature* 30, no. 3 (2003): 88–108. Other important essays on race and "Rue Morgue" include Nancy Harrowitz, "Criminality and Poe's Orangutan: The Question of Race in Detection," in *Agonisties: Arenas of Creative Contest*, edited by Jane Lungstrum and Elizaebth Sauer (Albany: State University of New York Press, 1997); and Lindon Barrett, "Presence of Mind: Detection and Racialization in 'The Murders in the Rue Morgue,'" in *Romancing the Shadow: Poe and Race*, edited by J. Gerald Kennedy and Liliane Weissberg (New York: Oxford University Press, 2001), 157–76.

48. Elise Lemire, "'The Murders in the Rue Morgue': Amalgamation Discourses and the Race Riots of 1838 in Poe's Philadelphia," in *Romancing the Shadow*, 184.

49. Lemire, 183. Her source for the detail about the Peale's Museum exhibit is Charles Godfrey Leland, *Memoirs* (New York: Appleton, 1893). Leland fondly recalls visiting Peale's Museum as a child—"And the stuffed monkeys—one shaving another—what exquisite humour, which never palled upon us!"—before noting that "'stuffed monkey' was a by-word, by the way, for a conceited fellow" (38).

50. Lemire, 195.

51. Thomas, 278.

52. See Quinn, 340; Silverman, 174–75.

53. Silverman, 174. Graham's income was estimated at fifty thousand dollars per year in the 1840s, according to Joseph Jackson, *Literary Landmarks of Philadelphia* (Philadelphia: David McKay Company, 1939), 150.

54. Quoted in J. H. Whitty, "Memoir," in *The Complete Poems of Edgar Allan Poe* (Boston: Houghton Mifflin, 1911), xliii; Thomas, 442.

55. Phillips, *Edgar Allan Poe the Man*, 1:749. Here Phillips drew on an unpublished manuscript, "Poe's Philadelphia Homes," by Philadelphia historian Ellis Paxson Oberholtzer, who interviewed several people who had lived near Poe. Oberholtzer's manuscript is apparently lost.

56. Elizabeth Milroy, "Assembling Fairmount Park," in *Philadelphia's Cultural Landscape: The Sartain Family Legacy* (Philadelphia: Temple University Press, 2000), 72–73; Phillips, 746–48.

57. John E. Reilly, "A Source for the Immuration in 'The Black Cat,'" *Nineteenth-Century Literature* 48, no. 1 (1993): 93–95.

58. See Armiento, 135–36; and Jason Haslam, "Pits, Pendulums, and Penitentiaries," *Texas Studies in Language and Literature* 50, no. 3 (2008): 268–84.

59. Oberholtzer, quoted in *The Rose-Covered Cottage of Edgar Allan Poe in Philadelphia* (Philadelphia: Anthony J. Frayne, 1934), 2.

60. *Rose-Covered Cottage*, 2.

61. Phillips, quoting Poe's neighbor Lydia Hart Garrigues, who was interviewed by Oberholtzer.

62. The North Seventh Street house's cellar evokes the murder scene of "The Black Cat"; though it was published in August 1843, Poe probably wrote the story before moving from Coates to North Seventh Street, according to Mabbott (TS 2:848).

63. Thomas, 877, 881.

64. *Rose-Covered Cottage*, 10.

65. W. J. Rorabauch, *The Alcoholic Republic* (New York: Oxford University Press), 8.

66. Geffen, 335; *Rose-Covered Cottage*, 12.

67. Geffen, 342; Thomas, 158. Burton did not mention Poe by name but referred to "the person whose 'infirmities' have caused us much annoyance," at a time when most subscribers would know that he was referring to his former coeditor.

68. Thomas Dunn English, "Reminiscences of Poe [Part 2]," *Independent*, October 22, 1896, 3–4 (accessed at www.eapoe.org).

69. English, "Reminiscences of Poe [Part 2]," 3.

70. Thomas and Jackson, 371.

71. Thomas and Jackson, 405.

72. Thomas, 534.

73. Silverman, 193–95; Thomas, 533–34.

74. Thomas and Jackson, 433–34.

75. Thomas and Jackson, 420–32.

76. Quinn, 401–2. Tomlin sent Poe the letter, which ended Poe's friendship with Wilmer.

77. Thomas and Jackson, 452.

78. Thomas and Jackson, 441–51.

Chapter 4: New York (1844–1848)

1. Edwin G Kenneth T. Jackson and David S. Dunbar, eds., *Empire City: New York through the Centuries* (New York: Columbia University Press, 2002), 102.

2. Campbell Gibson, "Population of the 100 Largest Cities and Other Urban Places in the United States: 1790 to 1990," US Census Bureau, http://www.census.gov/population/www/documentation/twps 0027/twps0027.html (accessed June 25, 2018).

3. David M. Henkin, *City Reading: Written Words and Public Spaces in Antebellum New York* (New York: Columbia University Press, 1998), 33.

4. Edwin G. Burrows and Mike Wallace, *Gotham: A History of New York City to 1898* (Oxford: Oxford University Press, 1999), 600.

5. Eric Homberger, *The Historical Atlas of New York City*, rev. ed. (New York: Henry Holt, [1994] 2005), 82.

6. Burrows and Wallace, 565.

7. Bayard Still, *Mirror for Gotham: New York as Seen by Contemporaries from Dutch Days to the Present* (New York: Fordham University Press, 1994), 99.

8. Still, 127.

9. Burrows and Wallace, 694–95.

10. See Kenneth A. Scherzer, *The Unbounded Community: Neighborhood Life and Social Structure in New York City, 1830–1875* (Durham, NC: Duke University Press, 1992) 19–24.

11. Still, 159–60, 143.

12. See Harold H. Scudder, "Poe's 'Balloon Hoax,'" *American Literature* 21, no. 2 (May 1949): 179–90.

13. A search on the *American Periodicals Series* database yields other examples from 1844–45, including the *Lowell Offering*, the *Christian Reflector*, and the *New York Observer and Chronicle*.

14. "New York Letter Writers," editorial, *Herald* (New York), February 28, 1844, 1.

15. See Scott Peeples, "'To Reproduce a City': New York Letters and the Urban American Renaissance," in *Poe and the Remapping of Antebellum Print Culture*, edited by J. Gerald Kennedy and Jerome McGann (Baton Rouge: Louisiana State University Press, 2012), 101–22.

16. Although they already knew each other's work, Poe introduced himself to Willis in a letter dated May 21, 1844, three days after the publication of the first "Doings" installment (Thomas and Jackson, 462). See also T. O. Mabbott's introduction to *Doings of Gotham*, xvii. On Poe's relationship with Willis, see Scott Peeples, "'The *Mere* Man of Letters Must Ever Be a Cypher': Poe and N. P. Willis," *ESQ* 46 (2000): 125–47.

17. On August 2, 1845, Poe published, in the *Broadway Journal*, a revised and expanded version of his sketch "Peter Pendulum, the Business Man," not only shortening the title and changing the narrator's name but also adding six paragraphs and making dozens of small revisions. The fact that Poe took this much interest in the story, rather than simply dumping a lightly revised text into the *Journal*, suggests that on Broadway in 1845 he saw a heightened relevance for

its satire of the business world and descriptions of comically exaggerated petty swindles.

18. See, for instance, Phillips, *Edgar Allan Poe the Man*: "Poe no doubt thought country air would help Virginia and benefit them all" (882).

19. Mary Maloney Brennan, quoted in William Fearing Gill, *The Life of Edgar Allan Poe* (New York: Appleton, 1877), 149, 150 (accessed at www.eapoe.org).

20. James R. O'Beirne, quoted in "Poe and 'The Raven': Circumstances Recounted to Prove Where He Wrote the Poem," *Mail and Express*, April 21, 1900, 1.

21. The case for Poe's authorship of this sketch, "A Moving Chapter," is not conclusive, but the evidence is strong enough to have earned Thomas Ollive Mabbott's acceptance.

22. Kenneth T. Jackson, *Crabgrass Frontier: The Suburbanization of the United States* (New York: Oxford University Press, 1985), 35. Jackson's description of omnibus travel is consistent with the impression made by Poe's satire.

23. Maura D'Amore, *Suburban Plots: Men at Home in Nineteenth-Century American Print Culture* (Amherst: University of Massachusetts Press, 2014), 83. Throughout the book, D'Amore discusses several antebellum male writers who in various ways promoted the new suburban ideal.

24. This letter is the crucial evidence that Poe moved in late January or early February. A letter dated March 20 includes the address 154 Greenwich Street (L 2:500).

25. In a letter to James Russell Lowell dated May 28, 1844, Poe lists five of these then-unpublished stories among his completed tales: "The Oblong Box," "The Premature Burial," "The Purloined Letter," "Mesmeric Revelation," and "'Thou Art the Man!'" He also lists "The System of Doctors Tar and Fether," which was not published until 1845. Since he had been living in New York only about six weeks at the time, it seems likely that some or all of these stories were written in Philadelphia.

26. Thomas and Jackson, 437.

27. John Ward Ostrom, "Edgar A. Poe: His Income as Literary Entrepreneur," *Poe Studies* 15 (1982): 5.

28. "Poe and 'The Raven,'" 1.

29. Thomas and Jackson, 495.

30. Thomas and Jackson, 497.

31. Thomas and Jackson, 491.

32. See Scherzer, 25–26, 49–50.

33. Thomas and Jackson, 498.

34. Thomas and Jackson, 497.

35. See Edward L. Widmer, *Young America: The Flowering of Democracy in New York City* (New York: Oxford University Press, 1999), especially 70–71 and 107–8; Meredith McGill, "Poe, Literary Nationalism, and Authorial Identity," in *The American Face of Edgar Allan Poe*, edited by Shawn Rosenheim and Stephen Rachman (Baltimore: Johns Hopkins University Press, 1995), 271–304; and J. Gerald Kennedy, *The American Turn of Edgar Allan Poe* (Baltimore: Edgar Allan Poe Society & the Library of the University of Baltimore, 2001).

36. Thomas and Jackson, 507.

37. According to Perry Miller, for instance, "All February and March the Longfellow business was the talk of a town that had little but politics to talk about" (*The Raven and the Whale: The War of Words and Wits in the Era of Poe and Melville* [New York: Harcourt, Brace & World, 1956], 129). See also Sandra Tomc, "Edgar Allan Poe and His Enemies," in *The Oxford Handbook of Edgar Allan Poe*, edited by J. Gerald Kennedy and Scott Peeples (New York: Oxford, 2019), 559–75, for more on Poe's strategic use of personal literary warfare.

38. Thomas and Jackson, 515–16.

39. Thomas and Jackson, 513.

40. "Introductory," *Broadway Journal*, January 4, 1845, 1.

41. Thomas and Jackson, 528.

42. Thomas and Jackson, 536.

43. Silverman, 259–61.

44. Phillips, "Poe-Plan of New York City," endpaper of *Edgar Allan Poe the Man*.

45. Thomas and Jackson, 582.

46. *Chivers' Life of Poe*, edited by Richard Beale Davis (New York: Dutton, 1952), 61. Chivers first heard from Maria Clemm that Poe had been at home "in bed for a whole week . . . pretending to be sick," then, on a visit the next day, witnessed it himself.

47. Thomas and Jackson, 529.

48. Thomas and Jackson, 622.

49. John Ward Ostrom, "Edgar A. Poe: His Income as a Literary Entrepreneur," *Poe Studies* 15 (1982): 5.

50. Thomas and Jackson, 625.

51. Phillips, 2:1110–11.

52. Reginald Pelham Bolton, *The Poe Cottage at Fordham*, Transactions of the Bronx Society of Arts, Sciences, and History, vol. 1 (n.p., 1922), 2.

53. John Carl Miller, *Building Poe Biography* (Baton Rouge: Lousiana State University Press, 1971), 101.

54. Thomas and Jackson, 640.

55. Thomas and Jackson, 641.

56. Sarah Helen Whitman, *Edgar Poe and His Critics* (New York: Rudd & Carleton, 1860), 31–32.

Chapter 5: In Transit (1848–1849)

1. Miller, *Building Poe Biography*, 163.

2. Thomas and Jackson, 726.

3. Silverman, 350.

4. Thomas and Jackson, 750.

5. Quoted in Christian Wolmar, *The Great Railroad Revolution: The History of Trains in America* (NY: Public Affairs, 2012), 51.

6. John F. Stover, *American Railroads*, 2nd ed. (Chicago: University of Chicago Press, [1961] 1977), 31.

7. See George W. Hilton, *The Night Boat* (Berkeley, CA: Howell-North, 1968), 65.

8. Thomas and Jackson, 757.

9. James Russell Lowell, *Lowell's Complete Poems* (New York: Houghton, 1898), 142.

10. Quoted in John E. Reilly, "Poe in Pillory: An Early Version of a Satire by A. J. H. Duganne," *Poe Studies* 6 (1973): 9.

11. Thomas and Jackson, 786.

12. Silverman, 414.

13. See Silverman, 414.

14. John Sartain, "Reminiscences of Edgar Allan Poe," *Lippincott's* 43, no. 3 (1889): 411–15 (accessed at www.eapoe.org).

15. Thomas and Jackson, 817.

16. Silverman, 419, 422; Semtner, *Edgar Allan Poe's Richmond*, 105.

17. Semtner, *Edgar Allan Poe's Richmond*, 92.

18. Susan Archer [Talley] Weiss, "The Last Days of Edgar Poe," *Scribner's*, March 1878, 714 (accessed at www.eapoe.org); Weiss, "The Sister of Edgar A. Poe," *Continent* 3, no. 6 (June 27, 1883): 818 (accessed at www.eapoe.org).

19. Susan Archer [Talley] Weiss, *The Home Life of Poe* (New York: Echo Library, [1907] 2011), 85.

20. See Poe's letters to Maria Clemm, August 29, 1849 (L 2:830–32) and September 18, 1849 (L 2:837–38).

21. "She Lives Over an Evening with Poe," *New York Herald*, February 19, 1905, 4 (accessed at www.eapoe.org); Thomas and Jackson, 832–33.

22. Thomas and Jackson, 839.

23. Quinn, 629.

24. Thomas and Jackson, 844. The quotation is Snodgrass's reconstruction of the note.

25. On these possibilities and additional careful research on the events leading up to Poe's death, see Matthew Pearl, "A Poe Death Dossier: Discoveries and Queries in the Death of Edgar Allan Poe," in two parts: *Edgar Allan Poe Review* 7, no. 2 (2006): 4–29; and 8, no. 1 (2007): 8–31. Pearl argues that Neilson Poe's account of Poe being returned to Baltimore by train is much more plausible than the "cooping" theory, though they were often presented together in biographical accounts.

26. "Edgar A. Poe: Zolnay's Bust of Him Unveiled at the University of Virginia—Mr. Mabie's Address," *New York Times Saturday Review*, October 14, 1899, 698.

27. Semtner, *Edgar Allan Poe's Richmond*, 114–18.

28. "History of the Cottage," Bronx County Historical Society, http://bronxhistoricalsociety.org/poe-cottage/history-of-the-cottage/ (accessed June 3, 2019).

29. "The House through the Years," Edgar Allan Poe National Historic Site, National Park Service, https://www.nps.gov/edal/learn/historyculture/timelines-house.htm (accessed June 4, 2019).

30. William Carlos Williams, *In the American Grain* (New York: New Directions, [1925] 1956), 216, 219, 220.

Index